Light In Darkness

A SURVIVOR'S STORY

BY

SIMON STERLING

AS TOLD TO

PHYLLIS STERLING JACOBS

Phyllis Sterling Jacobs

ISBN 978-0-9762033-0-8

LCCN 2005901808

This book is dedicated to my brother Zygmunt Sterling,
who died in the Brody ghetto, Poland in 1943 at the age of six.
May his memory be a blessing.

PHYLLIS STERLING JACOBS

Light In Darkness

TALMUD

When Adam saw for the first time the sun go down, and an ever deepening gloom enfold creation, his mind was filled with terror. God then took pity on him, and endowed him with the divine intuition to take two stones – the name of one was Darkness and the name of the other Shadow of Death – and rub them against each other, and so discover fire. Thereupon Adam exclaimed with grateful joy: "Blessed be the Creator of Light."

CONTENTS

SIMON STERLING, HIS WIFE SOPHIE, AND DAUGHTER PHYLLIS,
PHILADELPHIA, 1952.

Acknowledgments

I am so fortunate that my father, Simon Sterling, of blessed memory, at the age of 80, had the strength, courage and incredible memory, which allowed this story to be told. I am extremely grateful that, as he did throughout his life, he responded to what I needed, and in this telling left me with an incredible treasure.

Although my mother, Sophie Sterling, of blessed memory, could not talk about the losses she endured, I know she would be happy to see how the process of publishing this book has helped me come to terms with my experiences as a child of Holocaust survivors. I also believe she would be pleased that a part of her life's story is finally told. Her wishes for me to find my own way have always provided light, and have guided me in the creation of this book.

My heartfelt thanks go to Joyce Eisenberg, who recognized the beauty and value in keeping this book in my father's words and edited it with a masterful artist's fine brush. Her calls to me during the editing process, saying, "What your father does or says here is just amazing," let me know that the manuscript was in good hands. I am also grateful to Joyce for her patience, encouragement and excitement in being a part of this project.

My gratitude goes to Haim Coler, of blessed memory, for reading into a tape recorder letters written in Yiddish by my family, and to Dr. Dan Perlmutter for translating those letters into English. They gave me an incredible window into my parents' lives before and after the Holocaust.

I thank Sara Hodgson for patiently and artfully preparing the manuscript for publication, Jack Wellerstein for writing a wonderful teacher's guide and Ann Weiss for generously sharing her enthusiasm and expertise.

I greatly appreciate the support of many friends who are rejoicing with me at the publication of this book. I thank them all, and in particular, my cousin Betty Rice and Lumi Shapp, of blessed memory.

Special thanks go to my husband, Marc, who knew and loved my father and encouraged me to publish his words. To my children, Sara and Simone, who unfortunately did not know my parents, I pass on their grandfather's words, which I hope will be a guide for them throughout their lives.

SIMON STERLING IN FÖHRENWALD, A DISPLACED PERSON'S CAMP, NEAR MUNICH, GERMANY, 1948.

A Daughter's Story

My father had a story to tell, and after forty years, he told it to me. Now, after another twenty years, I am telling it to you. Some stories take a long time.

This book was not written by me or my father. Rather, it is a transcript of taped conversations we had about his and my mother's life – during and after the Holocaust. We taped over a period of several months in 1984, at which time my father was 80 years old. He died two years later.

The transcript of the tapes has been carefully edited only to clarify points and eliminate repetition. Mostly, these are my father's words as he spoke them. Although I am present throughout as a listener, I barely spoke during the taping and my voice is not heard in this telling. Through this book I am introducing you to my father. Once you've met him, I hope he will stay with you as he has with me.

My parents, Simon and Sophie Sterling, knew each other since they were teenagers. They grew up in the same town, Szczurowice, near Lvov, which was then in Poland and now is in the Ukraine. They were married in 1937, and had a son, Zygmunt, who was 5 years old when the Nazis invaded their town in 1941. They lived near extended family, consisting of parents, brothers, sisters, aunts, uncles, cousins, nieces and nephews.

Of my family living in Poland, only my parents and two of my uncles survived the Holocaust. My brother, who was 6 when he was killed in the Brody ghetto, is barely alluded to in this account. He is the one person I knew my parents could not tolerate to talk about.

Actually, I did not know I had a brother until I was 34, when I asked my father if I ever had a sibling. He turned pale, told me his name and age, and asked me never to say a word about him to my mother. I never asked about Zygmunt again.

I was born in 1946 while my parents were living in Föhrenwald, a displaced person's camp in Germany. It would be three years before we were admitted to the United States. When we settled in Philadelphia in 1949, my father was 44, my mother was 41, and I was almost 3.

My father begins his story with the Nazi invasion of his town, Szczurowice, Poland, in 1941. He describes his life in the Brody ghetto; his escape from a death camp in Zloczow, Poland; his keeping cover in a Christian friend's barn; and his year of hiding with my mother in the vast woods of Poland. He continues with their lives after the war in Russia, in a displaced person's camp in Germany, and then in the United States as immigrants.

My mother had died two years before I asked my father to do these interviews. She never talked to me directly about her experiences and losses, and I knew never to ask. Even when she smiled, it seemed to me that she was crying. She had an incredibly beautiful voice, but I rarely heard her sing. I couldn't bear adding to her pain with my questions. I realize now that I was also afraid of what I might hear, as I knew she was haunted by unthinkable memories. I recall that once when I was a child, she screamed out, "They killed him in front of me." I was too terrified to even think of who that person might have been. But, that memory, held for thirty years, prompted me to finally ask my father if I ever had a sibling.

By trying to protect both my mother and myself, I missed the possible opportunity of comforting her in her isolation. I deeply regret that in our mutual silence I could not console her in her grief or assuage her intolerable feelings of guilt for surviving. I wish I could say to her now, "It wasn't your fault." I wish I could hear her story.

When I asked my father to tell me his story on tape, to my surprise, he agreed without hesitation. Although I felt the emotional toll of the Holocaust from the air I breathed growing up in my home, the details – the people, places and dates – were like pieces of a puzzle floating around my head. I wanted to put the pieces together in one spot and look at the whole picture. After so many years of silence, my father was ready to talk. And I was ready to listen.

We sat at his dining room table with a tape recorder going, sometimes for an hour, sometimes for only 15 minutes. We stopped when he couldn't say any more. I very much wanted a clear chronology, so each time before we began again we would rewind to hear where he had left off. He spoke with little hesitation as if he had been preparing for years in his head to finally tell his story.

At the time I was relieved that he spoke without prompting, and I was reluctant to probe with questions I feared might have been too painful for him to answer – and for me to ask. Despite the fact that we were doing this taping, as we sat facing each other, I knew we were still intent upon protecting each other from the deepest pain. To my great regret, I never asked my father, during the taping or after, to tell me more than he offered.

Today our conversation would be different: I would ask him to tell me about our family, especially my brother. I would cry with him and hope that our shared grief would bring him some comfort. I would ask him to try to explain how he maintained his integrity, faith and optimism. I would tell him how grateful I am to him for leaving me with this incredible account.

While visiting my cousins in Israel, I was fortunate to discover a stack of old letters, which were written by my mother, father and Uncle Isak to my Aunt Nechama, my father's sister, who had immigrated to Israel before the war. These letters were written in Yiddish from 1945 through 1949 immediately after the war while my parents were waiting to immigrate to the United States. I finally had in my hands a real piece of the puzzle. Some of those letters are included in this book.

My father's story is an account of maintaining one's humanity in a world gone mad. It is a chronicle of love, commitment, courage, faith, hope and mindfulness in the midst of incredible losses and trauma. It is also an immigrant's story of making a place for himself in an optimistic and much-appreciated America, while secretly bearing the nightmares of a beautiful world ripped apart.

To the reader, it is my wish that as the layers of this book unfold you will come away from it changed – with a deeper understanding of our potential for strength, hope and courage, and a greater appreciation of how we nourish these gifts in each other.

PHYLLIS STERLING JACOBS
FEBRUARY, 2005

SIMON STERLING RECORDING HIS STORY IN 1984.

SIMON AND HIS DAUGHTER PHYLLIS IN 1984.

PROLOGUE

I don't want to tell you this. I don't want to make you feel bad.
It's not your fault. Thank God I'm all right, you understand. Only it's
so hard, it's so hard to explain. It's unbelievable to get through. You
have a sentence for death, if only they catch you. And you run, and
every place where you are going there are enemies and enemies and
enemies, you understand? You hide from so many enemies.

Let's say somebody here in the United States is running away
from jail. He walks in the street. Is it your business? He walks.
Is it my business? It's nobody's business. Even if somebody knew
something bad about him, he might say to himself, "It's not my
business." But there in Poland, if you walked out, any little child you
saw was your enemy. Everyone was your enemy. How can you hide
from so many enemies?

It's very hard to explain this to people here. They cannot
understand. And a lot of times I had in my mind, maybe it's me –
maybe I cannot explain to them. Then I figured, no, I'm explaining
it plain. It doesn't go in their minds, because people here in the
United States, in this democratic country, cannot understand. It's
unbelievable. So how much you should tell them? I don't know.

But I'm going to tell you this.

Simon, his wife Sophie (on right), and Sophie's sister Pepe Reiss in Szczurowice, Poland, 1932.

1

'I Never Believed Them'

In September 1939, when the Germans invaded Poland, we were very scared because we knew what Hitler meant to the Jews. What we didn't know was that Hitler had made a pact with Stalin to divide Poland, and that our town of Szczurowice near Lvov in Galicia would go to Russia. We didn't know this until Yom Kippur of that year, when the Russian army came to us.

Our town of 300 families, and the whole eastern half of the country, was under the Russian government. We were very happy with the Russians because they were no good for anybody – and the Jews were included in this anybody. This was good for us. The Jewish people were treated like the Polish and the Ukrainians.

In June of 1941, the Germans attacked the Russians. The day after, the German army came through town with tanks and trucks and hundreds and thousands of soldiers. This went on for three weeks. Jewish people stayed in their houses; everyone was scared to go out on the street.

One day the Germans, with the help of the Ukrainians, knocked on the doors. *"Juden, heraus!"* (Jews, get out!) They shouted. They took us into the schoolyard. We were about 250 people, including wives and children. My brother, Isak, and his wife and his two children were there. They beat my brother so badly that blood from his head covered his body. The Germans were ready with their guns.

Meanwhile, a general arrived and asked what this was. They told him something that we didn't hear, and the general ordered us back to our houses. We returned to an empty house; our Ukrainian neighbors had cleaned out everything, even the dishes. From this day on, our troubles started.

After the army went forward, the SS Commando came. They gave orders that every Jew had to wear a 10-centimeter armband with the Star of David. Anyone caught without a band would be shot on the spot.

The SS picked one Jew, a man named Mechele, to carry out their orders. "You are the Judenrat (the Jewish council). We will give you orders and you have to fill them out. If you don't do it, you'll be shot with your wife and two children in front of the Jewish people."

The Germans ordered Mechele to go to the Jewish people and collect all the jewelry they had. All their furs should be given over, also. The people who had rings gave in their rings, and everyone gave in their furs if they had them. These things were collected and packed up. Where they were sent, no one knows. Mechele had a hard time. When he came to someone, he cried with them because he couldn't help himself. He was in a very bad situation.

When it got colder, the Germans took away all our feather blankets. This went on throughout the winter. The men had to go out every day to work, and the Germans beat them all the time.

Then the Germans started what they called 'actions.' Nobody really knew what was going on. Orders came that all Jews should be on the street at a certain place. Some hid. Some ran back to their houses and were dragged out; they were placed on wagons, which went to the railroad station. The Germans loaded them up and took them away to Belzec, an extermination camp. We never saw them again.

When they took away some people, they left others. They didn't touch them because they couldn't catch them all at one time, so they waited for another time. They divided it up for a few times.

Whenever I heard or saw something, like cars coming into town, I could never tell who it was. Maybe it was the SS, so I ran away. I took my wife, Sophie, and my 6-year-old son, and I ran. We ran. We slept overnight in a field. In the daytime I sent a Christian friend of mine to look around. If he found out that it was quiet, we would return. This happened many, many times. We slept in the woods, in the fields, and sometimes in a barn that belonged to Anton Lukasiewicz, a Christian farmer I knew. My wife always listened to me. She believed in me. We had known each other since we were about 13.

We lived next door to my wife's parents and sister. One day, my father-in-law and mother-in-law came to me. "What are you doing to our daughter? She sleeps in the fields at night and when she comes back, she looks so worn out," they said. They told me I was doing the wrong thing.

"Listen, it's your daughter," I answered. "If you feel that I'm not doing the right thing by having her stay with me, then try to do the best for her. After the war, I will come back, and I will be her husband and do the best for her."

When they heard me talk like this, they realized I meant what I said. They stopped telling me to leave her in the house.

The day after Sophie's parents spoke to me, I heard some German cars coming into town. We ran away again and stayed overnight in a field. The Germans made an action that night. They took about 120 Jewish people to the train.

The next day, I sent somebody into town to find out what happened. I heard that my wife's brother had been there, but he didn't see anybody from his family. The day after, when I went to Szczurowice, nobody was around. My wife's father and mother and sister were gone, and they never came back.

The Germans gave an order that every Jew who was left should go to the center of town. From there they would take us to a ghetto, to a town called Radziechov. They said we were going to work there. I never believed them.

SOPHIE STERLING (STANDING ON RIGHT), SOPHIE'S MOTHER BAILLE REISS (CENTER), WITH FAMILY AND FRIENDS, SZCZUROWICE, POLAND, 1933.

Standing left to right: Simon's sister-in-law Fruma Sterling, Simon, his sister Hanna, Baruch Zvi Fisch, Simon's wife Sophie and his brother Isak. In front are Yaacov and Clara, Fruma and Isak's children, Szczurowice, Poland, 1935.

2

The Brody Ghetto

I made arrangements with another Christian friend of mine. At night, he got a horse and wagon and he took Sophie, my son and me to a town called Brody. There was a ghetto there already with about 12,000 Jewish people. Those from small villages, the ones who were still alive, had been sent to Brody. It was very, very bad.

We arrived about 2:00 in the morning and snuck into the ghetto. I went to the Judenrat, to poor Jews who the Germans had put in charge. They assigned us to a block, where about 600 or 700 people lived. I was put in a 14-by-16-foot room with about 15 other people, including women and children. There was no place to lie down.
I found a little space for Sophie and for the child, and I slept in the hallway. I met cousins of Sophie's, Hannah and Yossel, and their children, too.

I was in the Brody ghetto for about four months. During this time, typhoid fever went through some of the buildings. The typhus was so bad that every day hundreds and hundreds of people died. The Judenrat hid this from the Germans. They could, because the Germans didn't come into the ghetto. They only watched from outside the ghetto; they had the Ukrainians come in. If the Germans found out that there was typhus in a block, they would shoot all the people in that block right on the spot. They would liquidate the ghetto in a minute, so that the typhus would not spread.

People were lying on the floor begging for water. They had such high temperatures, and no one was taking care of them. I had had typhus before, the Flecken typhus, when I was young. If you had it before, you're not afraid of it. A person gets this typhus only once in his lifetime.

I, and others like me, went around giving people some water.

When they saw the water, they begged for a little of it. I would go get it, and when I came back, some people were already dead. We had to take them outside; we dug graves so that the Germans wouldn't know, and we buried them. This went on for a long time.

To find some food was very hard. Anybody who snuck out of the ghetto by climbing a wall took the risk of being shot. Every day they shot people who did this. In some places, Gentile people from the outside came to the ghetto. If you gave them a pair of shoes, they would give you a piece of bread. If you gave them a gold ring, they would give you something more to eat.

We were registered when we came to the ghetto; the Judenrat had the names of all the Jews in the ghetto. If somebody was caught trying to escape, the Germans would kill the whole family.

If the Germans came around to kill the people, you'd want to have a hiding place. Maybe you'd survive. You didn't know; everything was maybe. So I tried to make hiding places. I was young, in my late 30s, and everybody wanted to be my partner. I accepted anyone who wanted to help.

I built a hiding place in the basement of a bombed out building. We knocked out a wall in the basement and then we made a cover so you couldn't tell that people were hiding in there. We didn't have any tools, so we did it with our hands. In a few days, somebody else told me, "Simon, come with me and let's build another hiding place." I agreed. In all, I made about four hiding places. I figured if something happens, I'll run to the closest hiding place. If I can't run here, maybe I can run there.

When I finished making each hiding place, I always took Sophie in secret to show her exactly where it was and how to get there. I would tell her, "Here's how you can go in, and this man is my partner, and if you see him running to a certain spot, you follow him." I told her this because I never knew if I'd be around.

One day the Germans gave an order for all Jewish men 12 years of age and up to come outside. If a man didn't come out immediately, they'd shoot him and his family. I knew they meant it, so I told Sophie that I was going. We didn't know what was going to happen. We knew that every time they made an order, it was no good. There was trouble. You could not run away.

They took us away. We marched to a big building that had belonged to the Polish army and we stood and waited. They started asking us questions: "Who's a mechanic?" "Who's a tailor?" I said I was machinist. We had a flourmill and I knew about machinery. They put me on the side. There were about 2,000 or 3,000 men there and they made different kinds of groups. This process took hours and hours.

While we were lined up, the Germans marked and counted the number of people in each group. Two young brothers were standing in one group and their uncle was on the other side in another group. The uncle walked over to the two brothers because the boys wanted him to be with them.

The Germans counted the groups one more time, before they were going to take us away. "In this group there is one missing. In here there's one more. Who walked over to the other group?" a German officer asked.

The uncle stepped forward and said, "These are my nephews and I want to go with them."

"*Raus!* Get out of line." They pushed the two brothers and the uncle in front of us and told them to strip. They were begging and begging.

"Get undressed," the Germans ordered. The three Jews stood there in their underwear. The Gestapo took a gun and called a soldier, who might have been a 19-year-old boy.

All my life, I'll remember their screaming. They were shot. Slowly, slowly, slowly they fell down.

They put us on trucks and took us to a camp in Zloczow, about 30 miles from Brody. I quickly learned this was a liquidation camp. They bring about 10,000 Jewish people here. They keep them a couple weeks. They have them dig holes. Two or four weeks later, they take them out and shoot them. And I am here. It is March of 1943.

I met some people I knew. One was a relative of Sophie's, whose name was Marder. He told me, "Simon, this is the last stop. From here you cannot go anywhere." I told him about my Gentile friend who had always reassured me, "If you are ever in trouble, come to us and we will help you."

Meanwhile, the Germans needed men to load iron onto a train

going to Germany. They took workers from the last group that had been brought in from the ghetto. I was not among them.

They sent me and the other machinists to work with a group of German mechanics inside the camp. We didn't go out on the street or outside of the camp at all. The German soldiers who I was working with didn't do any harm to us. Sometimes they gave me a cigarette, sometimes a piece of bread to eat. They were plain boys who happened to have been in the army. But the Gestapo would come around at night when we were finished work. They'd beat up some older people and some young kids.

This cousin Marder came to me and said, "Simon, try to run away from here. Try to get out." We couldn't get out. We couldn't do anything. He had some gold coins. He said, "Maybe you need some gold money." I didn't want to take it. I was afraid if they caught me with it, they'd shoot me. And I saw that if anyone did something out of the ordinary, the Gestapo would shoot him.

One time they brought three men in front of us; the men had been caught and put in a cellar. The Gestapo chose four people to dig graves for them. They shot the three men, and then they shot the people who dug the graves, and they pushed them in. We saw it all from the window. It was on a Sunday.

We knew that this was the last stop.

At the camp, they kept some women in a big building to wash clothes for the soldiers. We came back late from work one afternoon, and we didn't see any of the women. We didn't know anything about what happened until some people from the town, who had come in to work for the Germans, passed by and told us that all the women had been taken into the woods that afternoon and shot. They dug their own graves and the Germans pushed them in. They were mostly young girls.

I feel there cannot be any miracle here.

3

No Questions Asked

Everyone who was working had a piece of cloth on his shoulder. The men who worked on the railroad had a red piece; I was working with the Wehrmacht so I had a "W." It would be impossible to get out of here if I stayed on the inside, I decided. People who went to work on the railroad, outside of the gate, could have a better chance of escaping. If I could be in that group, I would escape somehow. Sometimes something can happen on the road.

So I planned that at 6:00 in the morning, when the group that went to the railroad started getting together, I would try to join them. They got up a little bit earlier than the other people.

One day it was raining like cats and dogs. The German who was holding the guns, who was marching the people out, told the guard at the main gate, "We're taking them out; we have 210 or 220 people." Everyone was standing in a line and being counted. It was raining so hard. I took off my "W" and I put on a piece of red cloth. I quickly stepped into this group.

A Jewish man from Brody was doing the counting. The Germans always picked a Jewish man to do the final count. He was a friend of mine before the war. He saw me, and he stepped next to me and he said very, very quietly, "What are you doing here?"

"Don't ask any questions," I said, and he walked away. He counted and he didn't count me in. He told the Gestapo the number and I wasn't in that number.

I had known this man would do the counting, but I didn't know whether or not he would count me in, or whether he would tell them I was in line. I didn't tell him beforehand that I would be there. If I had, he would have told me not to do it, because it would be placing his life in danger. He could be shot.

I knew that no one would count again because it was raining so hard. We marched to the gate, and the guard pushed the button and the gate opened up. We marched down a little street. On the left side of the street was a stone wall. On the right side were empty bombed out houses. I remembered seeing them when they first took us in the truck to the camp. The mud was 2 feet high. The Germans were walking alongside of us on a pavement. They had their raincoats on. Their hoods were over their heads almost completely because it was raining so hard.

I was marching in the middle of the row. I pushed someone over to the middle, placed him in my spot and I moved to the side. Then I moved back in line behind a soldier. I spotted a house with the door open. I took just one step and I was behind the door. The people who were marching didn't say anything; they were in the same position as I was. The Germans kept walking and walking. I was standing behind the door and they were going and going. I closed my eyes. I figured, in a minute I'll be shot. But they're going and going, and they passed by. They were out of sight.

I jumped into the basement. I was there a whole day, just lying in the basement. I had in my pocket a little piece of bread that they had given me before. I lay there throughout the night. The Germans had an order that any civilian who was on the street or outside of his house after 9:00 p.m. would be shot. It didn't matter if you were a Pole or a Ukrainian. It certainly didn't matter if you were a Jew. There were no Jews in the street. People knew it and no one went out.

I waited until about 10:00 or 11:00 at night. I didn't hear anybody or anything, so I went out. I went from one house to another. They were all bombed out. Farther down, there were people living in houses. I knew the road because I had been in Zloczow before. I knew that Brody was about 30 miles away.

There were no trucks, no one walking, and no one there. No Germans, no townspeople. I didn't trust the road so I walked in the woods. And I was going and going. I slept in the woods another night. I didn't have anything to eat, and the second night I went out again.

My mind was like this: I thought perhaps Sophie was still in the ghetto; I would go there and we would die together. I'll go to the ghetto and let's die all together.

Before I escaped from the camp, I had spoken to a Jewish man whose job was to go back and forth to Brody every day with a Polish driver to get eggs for the Gestapo. When the Jewish man was finished with his day, he would be with us in the camp. Sophie's cousin Marder was a friend of this man.

Marder told me, "If you have a chance, you can escape. Try." He spoke to this man, this Jewish man who brought the eggs, and said, "Listen, do something for Simon. He has a chance; he knows some people outside. He knows some people where he can hide and he's a strong man. And he can survive. From here nobody will survive."

So this Jewish man told me, "When you escape, it should be around 8 o'clock early in the morning. You can see from the camp," he pointed. "You will go there, and then you will go left, and then you will go right. In the town of Zloczow is a garage. And in the garage is a truck."

I was in the fields for a few days before I came to the garage. This Jewish man had told his Polish driver, "Take him," and he agreed. When the Pole saw me at the truck, I didn't have to say a word to him; he didn't have to ask me anything. He knew why I was there. I'm a Jew; he knows where I am and what I'm doing. My plan was to get to Anton Lukasiewicz, the Christian farmer who was my friend.

His little truck was filled with wooden boxes for eggs. He took out one box from the bottom and put it on the top, and told me, "You go in there." So I did.

The road was ups and downs and ups and downs. The truck jumped up and down and I lay there under the boxes. The boxes hit me in the head and the floor hit me in the back. I watched that I should not get hit in the head. I covered with my hands my head. I didn't care about the body, you know.

He drove about 30 miles and stopped at a hotel just outside of the Brody ghetto. The ghetto was already liquidated; nobody was there. But I still thought I should go into the ghetto; maybe I would find my wife and child.

There was a small camp near where we stopped. The Germans brought the Jews that they found here – some people who were hiding, who hadn't been killed. The people I saw in this camp were the ones kept alive to bury the Jews that they killed.

And I saw how these people looked – not like human beings. You can't believe what they looked like. They were mostly young people, but any young man there looked like an old man, like he was 50 or 60 years old. They were going with shovels and they could just pick up their feet.

I said to the driver, "Listen, you helped me till here; now take me out of the town."

"Get in," he said.

"Where? In the back?"

"No, sit up front with me. Sit straight," he ordered. I had a cap on the side of my head and he gave me a cigarette. He drove through the town of Brody. I saw the streets. I knew every little house on every street in this town. I saw some people who were not Jewish. I recognized them. They didn't see me because I was in the truck. He drove and drove, and I saw everything. He took me out of there. After we passed a Jewish cemetery near the road, he told me, "Now's the time that you have to get out of the truck." We were in the fields, two or three miles outside of Brody.

When I went back to Brody, I had hoped to maybe find my wife and child. But after what I saw there, I knew no one was left.

I was lying in the field the whole day and the sun was burning, burning. The field was full of corn. I picked some and took it into my mouth. I was waiting for the nighttime. It started to rain. And I thought about this Polish man – this driver, who took me from the town of Zloczow into Brody and then into the fields. He could take a chance with me because he didn't know me. If they caught him, he could say; "He jumped into my truck; I never saw him." But for the Jewish man who helped him unload the eggs, he could do nothing. This Polish man was responsible for him. If he helped him, the Gestapo would kill him. They were friends. He helped me because the Jewish man asked him to.

This was June the 18th, 1943. Never could I forget the date. Every year since, as long as I could tolerate liquor, I would get drunk on this day.

Eight days after I escaped from the death camp in Zloczow, the Germans liquidated the entire place. They dug graves and they took all the Jews out of the camp and killed them.

After the war, I was looking all the time for someone from the camp who was alive. There had been 8,000 Jewish people there. I looked to find one person, but I couldn't find anyone. Finally I met someone who told me about one man who remained alive. He probably jumped from the truck when they took the Jews out of the camp and into the woods to be shot. To the death place. Some others tried to escape, and they killed them; but this one was left alive.

Nobody came out of those camps alive. People don't understand that in our area, there were no concentration camps where people worked and stayed alive. All the Jewish people in our area, the Germans gathered them together and took them to death camps. They were all killed. Hundreds of towns, from Volhynia up to Przemysl, Lemberg, Zloczow, Brody, Szczurowice, Radziechov and Lopatin, were *Judenfrei*, Free of Jews. They cleaned out the Jews 100 percent.

STANDING LEFT TO RIGHT: SIMON'S SISTER-IN-LAW FRUMA STERLING, AN UNIDENTIFIED FRIEND, AND SIMON'S SISTER HANNA.

KNEELING: SIMON AND SOPHIE STERLING.

SZCZUROWICE, POLAND, 1935.

SIMON'S AND SOPHIE'S HOME IN SZCZUROWICE AS IT LOOKS IN 2004.

SIMON'S FLOUR MILL STILL RUNNING IN SZCZUROWICE.

4

In Anton's Barn

I set out for Anton Lukasiewicz's village. I was very hungry. At night in the woods I saw the light of another farmer's house and I crept under the house near the window. I knocked at the window – not a gentle knock, but a strong one. In a loud voice I shouted, "Don't make any light. Open the window and throw out bread. We are 40 people here. If you don't do it, your house will be in flames."

I stood to the side of the window. A woman came to the window, opened it and threw out a nice piece of bread. She closed the window. I jumped into the woods and my eyes became alive and stronger.

To get where I wanted to go, I had to cross a river. I'm a good swimmer. This was early in the morning, about 2:00. It was summertime. I swam over to the other side of the river in the dark.

I walked through the fields until I came to the small village where my friend Lukasiewicz lived. I went into his barn. I knew that in the morning, he would come in to see the cows and horses and take out some hay. I figured if I went outside and he saw me (all the Jewish people were gone from that area), he could get scared and I'd be lost again. So I made myself a pile of straw hay on the side of the barn near the door and covered myself. When Anton opened the door in the morning and came around, I'd jump forward. I'd be standing in front of the door so he couldn't run out. And that's what happened.

He came in and I called, "Anton, Anton." When he saw me, he fainted. I jumped on him. "Anton." He couldn't talk; he couldn't say a word. He looked at me finally. He didn't ask me too much. He knew the whole story about what was happening with Jews in that town.

"Simon, stay here. I'm going into the house and I'll get you something to eat." His wife, Franka, came back with him carrying some food. She had covered it to make it look like chicken feed, so the neighbors wouldn't suspect anything. She was just bringing food for the chickens.

They came in and closed the door. I told them what had happened to me, and they told me what happened in Brody, because their town was not very far from Brody. They told me that the ghetto was liquidated. I asked Anton if he heard something about my wife, and he said no.

I had always told Sophie, "When they take me away and you have a chance to escape, this Anton Lukasiewicz, he will help you." When the Germans were in our town, I took her many times to Anton's house. I showed her where he lived, how to get there. My mind was always working how to outwit the Germans. How to escape and how to hide.

They kept me in the barn over the day, and they covered me.

The next night they came and took me out of the barn. They had made a place for me in a little hut where they kept their corn. On top in the hut there was hay, and they put me up there and brought me food to eat and gave me a bucket. They took care of what I needed. I heard people pass by in the village, and they were talking among themselves about what had happened to the Jewish people in town. What happened here and what happened there. And I was listening to it.

I wanted to smoke a cigarette. A cigarette to me at that time was the biggest medicine. Anton had some tobacco leaves. He was afraid I would start a fire in the hay, so he gave me a big metal container for the ashes.

I was there up in the hay for 14 days and I asked him – I told him – "Maybe you'll find somebody from Brody and maybe you'll hear something, maybe they heard something, about what happened to my wife and child." He went one time to Brody. He came back and said, "Simon, there's no one left." I told him about a Christian girl in the town who my mother was friendly with. Maybe Sophie went to her. He looked for her but he didn't find anybody.

One morning Anton came around. He didn't have to come up into the hay. He just moved a piece of wood and there was a hole and we could talk. He said to me, "Simon, how come you escaped and you left your wife, Sophie?"

"I told you that I was in the camp and I left her in the ghetto," I said. And he made a strange type of joke with me. I couldn't quite understand what was happening. Then his wife came around and stood right outside near the cows. I told her that her husband had just been here. He had made a strange joke, and I didn't understand what he was saying.

"He knows what he was saying to you. Sophie is here!" she told me. They couldn't take me down in the daytime. They waited for the nighttime, and then they took me to Sophie. She was in the barn – alone without our child.

You should see how she looked. It was unbelievable what she looked like. It didn't matter. She started telling me how she got there, but I didn't want to hear anything from her. When she told me what happened in the ghetto, in the hiding place, and how so many people died, I said, "Sophie, don't tell me any more. We are here. I don't want to hear any more about what happened there. This will not help you and it will not help me. We have to try to survive here."

But I did hear her story.

When the Germans found Jews in their hiding places, they killed them. But they didn't find all of them. Sophie hid in the ghetto between two walls; there were 24 people in this hiding place. Some Gentile boys went looking to rob jewelry and found them. The Jews gave them what they wanted so the boys wouldn't tell the Germans where they were hiding. During the 14 days Sophie hid between the walls, six or eight of the 24 people died. Children died. They buried them under the hiding place.

When the ghetto was liquidated, the Germans killed most of the people they found, but they did keep alive some men and gave them the job of burying the Jews. One of these men was from our town and his sister was hiding with Sophie. He knew where they were and he would find a piece of bread here or there and bring it to them. He would bring them some water.

Then he was killed. The Germans killed all the people who were burying the Jews. They no longer needed them. A lot of people had thought that if they helped the Germans out, they would stay alive. But no one did.

How did Sophie get out of there? How did she find the farm?

After the ghetto was liquidated, it wasn't closed anymore. There were no more police around. Sophie went out at night. No one was moving around. She walked about 16 or 18 miles. At a time like this, a person is strong like iron.

Sophie couldn't swim over the water like I did, so she walked across the bridge. There was a German there, but he didn't ask her anything. She walked right by.

She didn't walk on the main road after that; she walked through the fields. She got to Lukasiewicz, where I was hiding. She said she never believed that she would find it. But she found it, right?

SOPHIE, (NEE REISS) STERLING TWO YEARS BEFORE SHE MARRIED SIMON, SZCZUROWICE, POLAND, 1935.

5

Into The Woods

We stayed in Anton's barn for three days. And I figured, if he could take us back to that little hut for corn it would be very good. But he didn't take us back there. I didn't ask any questions. There were no questions to ask.

On the third day, Anton came into the barn with his wife and he told us, "Simon, Sophie, we cannot keep you here. I have a wife and children. If they catch you here, they'll kill all of us." And he told me in front of Sophie: "You alone I would keep. I know they will not catch you. You will run away and escape. But if they catch Sophie, they will beat her up and she'll tell them that I took you in and that I hid you."

"Keep her and I will go," I told him.

"No," he said. "She has to go. Look for a place for her and I will keep you."

I had no other place, and I couldn't leave Sophie. So he told me the best thing for us to do was to go into the woods.

Anton made arrangements with the forest warden who lived in a house in the woods. Bednarczyk was his name. I had known him very well before. A very plain man. A good man. He was a good drinker and a good man. He promised Lukasiewicz that he would help us.

At night, when we went into the woods, Bednarczyk was waiting for us. "Come with me. Follow me," he said, and he took us deeper into the woods. That's how we started to live in the woods.

I had been thinking about going into the woods anyway. . .

Before we went into the woods, Lukasiewicz told me that Sophie's brother Michael had come to him twice to ask about me. Michael knew that they had taken me away from Brody to the camp in

Zloczow. At this time, I was hiding at Lukasiewicz's, without Sophie. But Lukasiewicz didn't want to tell Michael that I was in his barn. Maybe someone would see Michael coming to his farm at night, and if they caught him, he would talk. So he told my brother-in-law, "Don't come to me; I'm afraid. I don't know anything about Sophie or Simon." He gave Michael something to eat and he left.

"If Michael comes again, please tell him that Sophie and I are alive and in the woods," I told Anton.

That same night, Michael returned to the farm. Anton told him that we were alive, that we had been at his farm and we now were in the woods, but he didn't know where. He sent Michael to Bednarczyk, and the woodsman told him where we were hiding.

Michael came to us the very next night. He told us how he had survived. He had been hiding in the ghetto in Brody, but not where I was. He wasn't afraid for his family because he didn't have anybody anymore. His father, sister and mother had been taken to Belzec, where they were killed right away. At this time, he had only a girlfriend remaining; he was engaged to her.

Michael escaped with his girlfriend at night. He was not a good swimmer, so he had to walk across the bridge. He figured that nobody would be on the bridge late at night. He was wrong. A German guard caught them. He took them back to our small town and gave them over to the Ukrainian police, who locked them up overnight.

The next morning, the police took them out of the prison. One Ukrainian – I remember his name, it was Kusht – was the murderer. Unbelievable. He forced a farmer with a horse and wagon to take them out to the woods where he would kill them. From the little town to the woods was maybe a mile and a half. Michael's girlfriend told him in Yiddish, "You try to escape. If the Ukrainian takes the gun, I'll try to fight with him."

When they came into the woods, Michael jumped up from the wagon. The policeman lifted his gun. The girl grabbed the gun and started shaking it. In the meantime, Michael escaped into the woods. Kusht killed the girl. He ran after Michael shooting at him, but he couldn't catch him. She was killed, this girl there in the woods.

Michael had been in hiding with a Christian farmer about five or six miles from the woods. He stayed with us overnight and the next day because he couldn't go back to his hiding place until it got dark. And then I was just with Sophie in the woods. It was in the beginning of July 1943.

All the time the Germans made hunting parties – and not for animals. To find some Jewish people in the woods. They trained dogs to find the smell of people. They mostly called the people from the villages. The boys and the girls, they should go look for Jews. Bednarczyk the woodskeeper told me, "If this will happen, I will warn you. I'll let you know ahead of time."

The woodsman would come every couple of nights during this time, and he told us we should move around because the villagers would always be looking for us. We should never stay in one place because the smell of people would bring somebody in.

So we moved all the time. On my left and on my right were big woods for miles and miles.

About two weeks later, Michael came around at night; that same night Bednarczyk appeared. The Germans had let him and the other woodsmen know that they were organizing a hunt in all the villages in the area.

"You have to run," he told us.

"Where should be run to?" we asked him.

He told us about some swamps that were five miles away. "You have to go to there."

So we did – me and Sophie and Michael.

We hid in the swamps overnight. There was a lot of water. We took some of the leaves from the little trees. We tied them up together to make a little bed. We laid down, but the water came up through the leaves. What can you do?

Michael had a piece of bread in his pocket. When it became dark at night, I heard something moving around. It was a noise not of people but of certain animals. Rats. Big rats. The rats were jumping all over us. One rat smelled the bread and went into Michael's pocket. Michael caught it.

I didn't sleep. I was standing in the water near Sophie and keeping the rats off of her. When I heard something, I tried to push it away. It was some night.

We had to stay in the swamp the next day because in the daytime you can't go out. You can't move around. We waited for the night.

And the day was long like a year. A minute was like a day.

At night, we went back into the woods. We were covered with mud from the top to the bottom. We went to a little stream, took off our clothes and washed out the mud. We put them back on wet, but it didn't matter.

We didn't have anything to eat, and we were hungry. When Michael was hungry, it was murder. He wanted to go out in the daytime for food. I told him, "If you go in the light, you'll never come back, and we'll be in danger." A lot of times I was fighting with him. When he became hungry, it was unbelievable.

But Sophie never asked for food. She wanted to die.

The next night, Michael ran away to find food. I left Sophie and went back to Anton Lukasiewicz. To go to him was about three miles. I didn't go on the road; I walked through swamps and through the woods. I wasn't afraid at night. No people went out at night. Germans didn't go out at night, because they were afraid themselves.

When I came to Lukasiewicz, I didn't have to go into his house. When I came around his dog would start barking – not like I was a stranger, but like someone he knew. Lukasiewicz heard it and came out. "You are lucky," he told me. "The dogs brought the Germans and Ukrainians and the villagers to the place where you were lying the day before, and they couldn't understand where you disappeared to. They were looking for you for miles and miles. They were looking the whole day, and they didn't catch anybody."

Anton gave me something to eat and to bring back for Sophie – some milk in a bottle and vegetables. I also brought back a piece of bread.

I returned to her about 2:00 in the morning. She was lying there, not yet asleep. She was just lying there. I brought her the food, and she drank the milk and ate the bread and the vegetables. But a lot of times she didn't want to eat.

She started to talk. She didn't talk much. She said she wanted to die a natural death - not to get killed from the Germans.

"Sophie, God will help us. We will try," I told her.

6

Digging In

In the beginning, the weather was good. It was summertime, and in the gardens they had carrots. So we went into the gardens at night and took some. Later there were cucumbers and onions. We didn't go to one garden and take a lot; we went to different gardens and took a little from each. We tried not to make any damage to the gardens, so no one would know it was missing. We didn't want people to get mad.

I tried to go maybe once a week to catch some food. I went to Lukasiewicz. He always gave us food. And his wife was wonderful; she also gave us food. I could have eaten everything at one time, but if he gave me a piece of bread, I divided it. A piece for today, a piece for tomorrow, and a piece for the next day.

We were already so used to eating little. We were always hungry.

Two weeks later, Michael came back. He had told the farmer who was hiding him that Sophie and I were in the woods. The farmer said we could come to him for food. It was about five miles to go, but we went. You know, we had nothing to eat. We would go anyplace for something to eat.

Michael went inside to let the farmer know we were there. He told us we should hide in the woods, and his wife would prepare something for us to eat. She made a soup with milk and flour and potatoes. He brought out a big bucket with spoons.

Sophie, Michael and I sat in the woods and ate this soup. When was the last time that we saw soup? It was warm and it was good. We ate up everything completely. He brought us out a bread. This gave us a lot of strength.

The farmer gave me tobacco that he had grown himself. No matches; I made fire with a stone and a piece of cotton I tore from my coat. It took me half an hour. I smoked the tobacco, and then it was time to leave.

The woods I would describe like this: It's like there is no end. But we did know where we were and where we were going. We were walking on a path that was just big enough for a horse and wagon. It went on and on for about five or six miles. In some places it cut over a road. We didn't say a word among us. We just walked. I was on the right side, Sophie was in the middle and Michael was next to her. We were going slowly, going, going. We figured we'd go to a certain place where the woods were very dense, and that would be our hiding place.

Then I heard something. When you take an iron stick and brush it against dry little branches, the iron gives you a signal. It makes a certain noise. And you could hear something like that for a mile in the woods. The echo just travels. And I heard that. I touched Michael, and Michael touched Sophie and we stopped.

We heard another sound like that. We were sure that somebody was going there. Michael pushed Sophie next to me. He moved to the outside. I understood what he meant. If something was wrong, he would run into the woods. I felt it was dangerous, but I would not be able to run because I couldn't leave Sophie, and Sophie wouldn't be able to run after me. She couldn't run fast. She was weak, like a nothing.

So, I figured, I'm in danger anyway. Michael will run in the direction of the dense woods.

But dummy Simon. I had a wife; her life was my life. I figured if somebody was there, and he heard my voice, he would be scared – if it's just somebody from the village. I had nothing to lose, so I shouted in Ukrainian, "Give me your name."

"Give me your name"! I shouted again, in a big voice.

"Simon, Simon, it's me," a man hollered. It was my brother, Isak. He had recognized my voice. We came together. My brother was with Yossel Parnas, my sister's husband.

This was a miracle.

We all walked deeper into the woods, and we found an area where there were swamps. We picked a place that would be hard to get to, because we had to stay here over the day. In the middle of the swamp the ground was a little higher. We tested it to make sure it was dry.

We went in and sat down. This area was covered with branches, so it was hard to see us.

It was here that my brother told us what happened to them. He was in the Brody ghetto with his wife, Fruma, and two children. He had a boy, Yaacov, who was 16, and a girl, Clara, 12 years old. After they took me away from Brody to the liquidation camp, the Germans killed Yaacov and another few boys in the ghetto. My brother buried his son by himself.

His wife and daughter were alive and hiding in the ghetto. When the Germans liquidated the ghetto and found them, they took them out to the Jewish cemetery and killed them.

At the time his family was found, accidentally my brother was not in the same hiding place. He and Parnas were somehow not found.

The Germans had taken Parnas' family – my sister and their child – away from Szczurowice at the same time they took Sophie's parents and her sister. They took them all to Belzec camp where they were killed immediately.

My brother, Isak, and Yossel escaped from the ghetto together, and now they had a hiding place in a village not far from these woods. They were staying with a man Isak knew. A nice man. A poor man.*

They were tired of hiding in this man's basement. They wanted to go out a little bit, so they went away for a night and a day to be in the woods. They planned on going back to their hiding place the next night.

Then, accidentally, I found them in the woods. Can somebody believe that?

They stayed with us a whole day, and they told us everything that happened in the ghetto – so many big stories about what went on.

After this meeting, Isak and Yossel would sometimes come out to the woods to see us. This went on from July 1943 through the end of March 1944. During this time, the Germans were always making hunting parties in the forest. There were no more Jewish people around. No ghettos, nothing. Every place had been liquidated.

The only Jews alive were the ones in hiding places. On one

* *Stefan Miniewski, a Polish Christian, along with members of his family, hid Yossel Parnas and Isak Sterling on their farm. When news spread about how they survived, some Ukrainian nationalists murdered Miniewski for helping Jews. He was awarded posthumously the medal of "Righteous Among the Nations" by Yad Vashem.*

hunting party, the Germans caught young Jewish people from Szczurowice, my town. And they killed them there in the woods.

When we were in the woods, we slept one night in one place. The next night, we went a mile to another place. Sometimes we walked two miles, because the Germans had dogs that could smell a mile. If you stayed in one place too long, they would come with the dogs and catch you right away.

We always looked for woods that were short and spread around, that covered all of the ground. Under these woods grass doesn't even grow, because the ground is covered with young trees. Each branch was near the other. Everything was so close you couldn't be seen. These were the woods we were looking for – not high woods, where you could see people.

During the day, we hid. We lay buried up underground, under low branches, under bushes. When the sun beat down on us, there was no breeze. The sun burned like a fire. Sometimes in the daytime we would hear a noise and we'd think it was people. All of a sudden, we'd see that it was a wild animal. Then we started digging holes under the ground, so as not to lie completely in the open. We lined the holes with a few pieces of wood. We put leaves on the top for a roof.

When it's raining, the roof doesn't matter. The water goes in. It was often raining; we would get completely wet and we could not dry out. The heat goes from your body like steam from a chimney.

But there was no water to drink. No water. How much water can you carry? We had two bottles, like seltzer bottles. In the night we went to a swamp and put the bottles in the water. When you let the water sit, in a half an hour you have a quarter bottle of mud inside. The mud didn't bother us; we drank the water anyway.

In the morning, we had a little piece of bread and we drank a little water. The rest of the day we didn't have any water. The sun was starting to burn, and we had no water and no breeze. We undressed ourselves completely and still we were burning.

How we hated the daytime. The day was murder. It was so long, like a year. In the daytime it was very dangerous because always the Germans and the Ukrainian police were looking in the woods, and we were always afraid. We waited for the night.

The best thing was the night. We knew at nighttime we were much more safe. I prayed to God, "Why did you make the day? Night. Let it always be night." At night we could breathe because we weren't so afraid.

In the nighttime, I tried to make Sophie comfortable and keep her hopes up. I took leaves and put them under her; she should not have to lie on the ground. I had a hard time with her. She didn't care if she lived or died. She didn't talk too much.

One night, Michael came with more news. He had been hiding alone in a basement that belonged to some Gentile friends. The basement was dark and damp, and Michael wanted to get out. Someone in the woods connected him with Fischel Fisch, who was hiding in the woods with a woman named Pina Potash, her two young sons, Mendle and Motle, and her brother-in-law, Jacob. I knew them very well. I was a partner in the lumber business with the Potash brothers.

Pina and her husband, Lazar had escaped from the Brody ghetto along with their boys and her brother-in-law. When they passed through Szczurowice, our town, Lazar didn't want to go along with the rest of the family because he was afraid he would be recognized. So he walked separately from them through the woods. He was caught and killed.

The others weren't caught. A farmer who was riding by picked them up. Nobody paid attention to them. When they came to the woods, they went into hiding.

Michael said they were in another section of the woods, far away, maybe about six miles from us. It was dangerous to go there through certain roads, so we didn't go.

This Fischel, who was Isak's brother-in-law, was a very nice man, but he was not capable of helping the woman by himself. He was very much a slow poke. And Pina and Jacob wanted help. They were young people, but they just couldn't do it alone. They were lying on the ground in the same dense, young woods in a dangerous place.

Michael told them that Sophie and I were alive. And so was my brother, Isak, and my brother in-law, Yossel. Michael asked me to help Pina build an underground hiding place.

Isak came one night to the woods to meet me, and we made up

our minds. We would go over there some night, stay in the woods with them a whole day and make them a hiding place. We organized the shovel.

From Lukasiewicz I took a shovel. We needed a hand saw, a small one. My brother brought that. We didn't need any nails. We chose the night that we should go. It should be in miserable weather. Rain. It was always safer for us in miserable weather. We waited. I don't remember if it was in the middle or end of August, but we went there in the night and we started digging.

"Just dig a little hole," said Pina.

"If we're already digging, let's dig a large hiding place," I told her. Nobody knows what will happen. Nobody knows who will need it. I had this in my mind right away.

We made the hole bigger. When you make a hole, if you go deeper the earth will not move; it will stay. We made it about four feet deep and about half the size of our dining room. Everyone there was digging, even the children, and we made the hiding place. We were young and we did it.

Then we cut small trees. We put the trees on the top, and we put leaves over it. We made an opening to go in.

We were there over the day, but we didn't finish. We figured we'd come another time.

In another week or two, we finished it up. Fischel was there with Pina, her brother-in-law, Jacob and the boys. He told me, "Simon, I want to go with you."

"Fischel, I don't take anybody with me. Even if my brother wanted to stay with me, I would hesitate because it's dangerous. The smaller the group, the better. There cannot be too many people there," I explained.

I returned to my place in the woods. Soon after, Michael found for himself that he was better off with us. I wasn't too anxious for him to stay with us. But what could I tell him – no?

We moved, moved from place to place all the time, and there were always different things around us. The villagers came sometimes to cut wood. There were a lot of farmers coming into the woods. And children coming into the woods. We had to move and we had to run away from there.

We were cut off. We didn't know what was happening. But sometimes when Michael went out, he would come back with news. And when I would go to Anton Lukasiewicz, he told me what was going on in the war. He told me that the Russians were beating the Germans, but at this time the Russians were far away in Moscow.

My brother came one time with Yossel to stay overnight, and he told us that we should start preparing for the winter.

"Why do you want us to prepare now for the winter? It's still warm out. Now is too early," I told them.

"Let's try it now. It's warm outside and we can do some work," Isak said.

We went to talk with Bednarczyk, the woodskeeper. "What would you suggest that we do for the winter? What should we do?" we asked.

He suggested that we leave the place we had been hiding, because not far away there were big trees. In the winter there would be commercial business there, and that was no good. They'd come to cut down the trees for firewood.

Bednarczyk said he would take us to the swamps, to a certain area where it was higher and there were a lot of small trees. The trees were near each other, and it would be a good place to hide.

A couple of weeks later, Isak and Yossel returned to us, and we decided that we would go to the swamps and make a place. We dug out a hole and started to make something resembling a round wall oven, like the old-timers used for baking bread. That's what we started to dig.

And the earth! We couldn't put it out right there. We had cotton bags that the farmers had given us. We filled them with the earth that we were digging. We took them the equivalent of five or six blocks, and we emptied the bags in a hole in that area. This took a long time. There was so much earth, and you had to take each bag and fill it and bring it to the place to be emptied. The sacks weren't large; they were like the size of small mail bags.

It took us four or five weeks to make this place. We were working very hard. And we were weak. There was nothing around there; only the steps that we made. We could cover the steps with some little trees.

And on the top? We made the hole so that after we got in, we could put our hands out and get some branches and small trees still in earth to cover the entrance, and you couldn't see that the place was there.

Only you have to leave air. Air and water. These are the first things a person has to look for. Air and water. You cannot live without air and you cannot live without water. Without food you can live 10 to 12 days. And you're starving to death.

But when you don't have water – and you don't have air – in 10 minutes you're dead. So we dug little holes. We couldn't make big holes; we had to make little holes for air. A lot of times we were sitting by the hole and sucking the air in.

It was big enough for five people, and I don't mean five people standing up. It was big enough for five people lying down. You had to lie down.

There were five of us: me, Sophie and Michael made three. Isak and Yossel were going to stay here for the winter, too.

So, we made and we covered it. We wouldn't use it now. We'd keep it for the winter.

SIMON AND HIS BROTHER ISAK AT FÖHRENWALD,
A DISPLACED PERSON'S CAMP NEAR MUNICH, GERMANY, 1948.

7

'Every Minute Is A Year'

We returned to our hiding place, and my brother went back to his spot with the farmer.

One time, when Michael went to see the woman with the two children, Fischel begged him, "Please take me to Simon."

"I cannot take you to Simon," Michael said. But Fischel was begging and insisted. Michael agreed.

In the night, Michael brought Fischel to me.

"Michael, why did you do this? Fischel, what are you doing here?" I asked.

"It's a dangerous place there," Fischel replied.

"What are you doing here? It's dangerous here, too; I have Sophie with me."

He came. What could I do? Give him over to the Germans? So, that night I said to him, "Fischel, tomorrow we're going to go to a place and make a hiding place and we're going to dig a hole."

"All right," he agreed.

The next night, I left Sophie by herself and we went in the woods. I didn't tell Fischel about the hiding place that I had made with my brother and my brother-in-law. First of all, there was no place for him there. We dug another hole in the woods and made a hiding place for Fischel. And, oh, he loved it there. He would go out in the night to see a man who gave him a piece of bread. Fischel was a very dangerous person because he had a habit of coughing. He coughed all the time. I always grabbed him by the mouth and said, "Don't cough!" He tried, but he couldn't control himself.

It was still summertime, and we had vegetables from the gardens. Later on, there were apples. We had some food. You know, it was a life. I remember when I would go under an apple tree. I wouldn't go away until I had filled myself up. I would take as much as I could with me.

A lot of times I did leave the woods. I would go to Lukasiewicz's house and take Sophie with me. He never knew when I was coming. And I wouldn't tell him that I was there. I knew how to sneak into the barn. I would dig out a hole in the hay; I put Sophie in and we were sitting there. And we were lying there in the straw. I figured, let me stay here a few days. It's a little different than in the woods.

But when Lukasiewicz came to the barn to bring the cows some seed, he smelled us right away.

"Simon, where are you?" he would ask.

And I would say, "I'm here."

Anton and his wife would bring us food. Many times I cheated him. I told him I was going away to the woods, and then I went back to the barn and hid myself. Sometimes he knew it, and he didn't say anything. He didn't talk to me. He pretended he didn't know anything.

One day, Bednarczyk, the man who was taking care of the woods, found us and warned us that tomorrow the Germans were coming. They planned to take a lot of guards into the woods to look for partisans and Jews who were in hiding. That night we escaped from the woods and hid in Lukasiewicz's barn. In the morning he came in to take hay for the cows and the horses. He didn't notice us. He had a big pitchfork for the hay, and when I saw and heard that pitchfork near me, I thought he would finish me with it.

"Lukasiewicz, stop, stop. I'm Simon," I called. He got scared. I jumped up from the hay.

"It's good that you jumped up and that it's you, because I would have killed you," he said. I told him about Bednarczyk's warning and how we had to escape from the woods. We would just stay overnight.

Later, a Polish priest by the name of Stanislaw Mazak came to Anton's house. Lukasiewicz had told him in confession that he had been helping me with some food, and the priest told him he was doing the right thing. You see, Mazak knew me very well; I was friendly with him before the war. The priest was younger than me, maybe he was in his late 20s or early 30s. I belonged to the city council; my father was the head of the Jewish Community, so he was a councilman. He resigned and I was his replacement, and the priest belonged there, too. At this time in Poland, there was a lot of anti-semitism, but Mazak didn't show anything. He was a very fine man.

When I stayed in the barn in the daytime, I was always looking for holes in the wall where I could see what was going on outside. I was lying there a whole day and watching outside. Somebody could come – a stranger. I should know. I should think what I have to do.

I saw the priest come to his house, and Lukasiewicz probably told him that I was there. He didn't go inside to see me because he was afraid someone might see us. Mazak walked in front of the barn and he was singing. He was singing! I don't remember the song; in Polish, he was singing – slowly. He was going around and around the barn for about 10 or 15 minutes. And I was watching him. He knew that we were there, and he was singing to give us more hope. Something like this. Yes, he was a very fine gentleman.

When Mazak was walking away from the barn and away from the house with Lukasiewicz, he turned around and looked up at me in the barn. And then he left.

Sometimes Mazak made cookies and brought them to Lukasiewicz. He didn't say, "This is for Simon and Sophie." He came to him like a priest. He had the cookies in a paper or in a little box. But Lukasiewiez knew for whom he was bringing the cookies.

Anton's wife, Franka, was the best. One night I came to the house. I was hungry. It was Christmas Eve, but I didn't know it. Anton and Franka knew from the dog's bark that it was me. Franka came out of the house and coughed. This was the sign to tell me she was there.

It was Christmas, she told me, and there were a lot of people in the house – farmers from the town and relatives. Franka had me follow her into the back of the house, into the pantry. She gave me food and went back and forth to the farmers. They asked her who was there; she told them someone had walked by but left. She kept coming back to the pantry. They had a lot of food. She fed and fed me. I ate so much food, I fell asleep, and later she woke me up and made Sophie and me a package to take. Sausage, bread, so much food, and I left.

Before the war, when the Germans came into our town, I had

given Lukasiewicz clothes from Sophie and me to keep – some suits and my coat.

After the war, I took back my coat. Why not the rest? I couldn't ask for the rest. I appreciated them too much. I knew some people who went back to get things that Polish farmers and other people had hidden for them. When they went back to get their things, the Polish farmers killed them. And this was after the war.

When I left the ghetto, I had given Sophie a 20 dollar gold piece. She sewed it up in her clothes to hide it. I told Lukasiewicz, "I have a 20 dollar gold piece, and I'll give it to you. I know you give me your food, and the Germans are taking away most of the food. I will give you the 20 dollars. Sell it and buy me something to eat."

He was afraid to do this, he told me. Where could he sell the gold coin?

"You give Mazak the 20 dollar coin piece, and he'll exchange it for something," I told him.

Anton gave it to him. When the priest was in Brody, he sold the coin and he brought Lukasiewicz the money. Lukasiewiez bought food.

Money doesn't mean anything to me. You cannot buy from the trees. The trees don't talk and they have nothing to sell. So they bought food and they gave it to me. It was a good thing.

When I went to Lukasiewicz's to stay overnight or over the day, I didn't tell Fischel where I was going. I just told him I was going out. Sometimes I would bring him back something to eat. He was lying there alone. When he had a piece of bread, he wouldn't move. He would never go out.

This was going on for a long time, this running and hiding. It's very hard to explain. Every minute was a year. Every minute there was something unbelievable. I cursed the days every minute of my life. The day was the worst time. The sun is shining; you're in the woods; anyone can come around. Do you understand? There were planes flying around, small planes. We saw them; they couldn't see into the woods.

Fischel had a book, and in it he was writing down all the stories about what was going on. The book was falling to pieces. "Fischel, what are you writing?" I asked him. "Do you have to write? If you'll be alive, you'll remember; you don't have to write."

No, he told me. He had to write down every little thing: where he went, where I went, what happened here, what happened there. This book didn't survive. It turned to powder. I'm sorry it did.

FAMILY AND FRIENDS: (LEFT TO RIGHT) SIMON'S YOUNGER SISTER RACHEL, FISCHEL FISCH, HANNA BERNSTIEN, AND SIMON'S WIFE SOPHIE, SZCZUROWICE, POLAND, 1932.

Seated with their family are Anton and Franka Lukasiewicz in 1957. Anton and Franka were honored by Yad Vashem as "Righteous Among the Nations" for the courageous help they extended to Simon and Sophie during the Holocaust.

8

The Whole Winter

In Europe, the winter is winter. We decided that when the first snow came, we would go to Lukasiewicz. I talked it over with him. When we come before the snow, I asked, could he please prepare something more for us? Something more to eat, so we wouldn't have to go out from this hiding place for three or four weeks.

I asked Fischel what he planned to do for the winter. He knew that we had a place, but he decided to go back to Pina, Jacob and her children. Michael went to his place, to his farmer.

One night, toward the end of January, I saw it starting to snow. A nice snow. When the snow is falling in the woods, it's not windy. In Poland, snow falls like a bricklayer laying bricks. It can go on for a whole week. You're up to your neck in snow, and it's so cold.

I went to Anton's house. The first thing he gave me was some whiskey; so I drank. He gave me something to eat in the barn, like always. He and Franka had prepared everything. They gave me a bag with two strings, like a knapsack.

I started back. I was walking in the middle of the road when the snow stopped falling. I knew this would be the worst thing because I would make footsteps. Footprints are no good. This is what happens: Rabbits don't like to spring on the snow, so they spring on footprints. When the farmers go out to make wire traps to catch the rabbits, they see the footprints. The people who lived near the woods were always looking for signs of people hiding.

When I got back to our hiding place, it was already getting light; morning was coming. We stayed inside the hiding place the whole day, thinking about those footprints.

I went out in the afternoon and gave a look. I saw new steps, new footprints on the side. And it wasn't ours, because we knew our footprints. We used to walk backwards; if you want to hide footprints, you walk backwards. It looks like someone is going out, not in. But I had walked a very long way. How could I go backwards with so many things to carry?

We came out and we saw it was no good. Nobody would be in the woods yet, because it takes time before they tell the police. . . until the Germans come. It's a large wood.

In the meantime, we heard Bednarczyk. He was coughing, which was our signal that it was him. He told us to come out. We already knew what had happened and what he was going to tell us.

"You know what I should do to you? I should kill all of you. Because look what you did; you made footprints in the snow, and boys saw the footprints and found out – found you, and they went and told the Ukrainian police. The Ukrainians told the Germans, and for tomorrow morning, they're organizing a hunting party," he said.

They knew that here was Jewish hiding.

"Run where you can; I cannot tell you where. It's winter, it's snow," he told us before he went away.

We were ready, prepared to run. My brother, Isak, had the place where he was staying before, with my brother-in-law Yossel. Michael had a place where they'd let him in. Only Sophie and I didn't have any place where to go. I knew Lukasiewicz would not let me in, because he knew they were looking for us. So, we're sitting and thinking.

"Simon, you know I'm sorry," Isak began. "I would take you where I am, but there's only space for two people. It's a hole in the basement."

And I told Michael, "Michael, come here. This is your sister and my wife, and you know that I'm doing everything to help her survive. Take her with you. When everything quiets down, I'll take her back." But, the farmer would only hide one person.

I'm alone with Sophie. Only in my mind, I had it right away. I thought, wait a minute. I helped make a hiding place for the woman and her two children. And it's a nice snow and it's cold. I thought about the food that we had there inside and how much we could take with us.

I took Sophie on my shoulders. She couldn't move. I fell down and picked her up and fell down again. It was about six miles minimum. And you're not going on the road. You're going in the woods and you're going in the snow.

So I'm going and going and going. The woods are so dense, and I pushed myself through them. Everything was frozen. Sophie was so broke down. She didn't weigh too much. She was frozen on her hands.

When I made this hiding place, I had counted the steps. How many steps to the lane? How many steps from the lane to the main road? Today I don't remember, but then I remembered every little thing. I counted the steps because I figured if I missed the hiding place, I'd be a dead person. The cold was so freezing. The cold would eat me up, especially with Sophie. There was a tree; a strange-looking tree. You cannot make a mark on a tree because a tree will be cut down, so I made a mark in my mind. So when I saw the funny tree, I knew that I was all right.

I'm fine, I figured. I have to make about 15 or 18 more steps. There around should be the place. And there was a little empty space. I took Sophie and I put her down. I didn't really put her down. I just shook my shoulders and she fell down in the snow. I knew in the snow she couldn't get hurt.

I took out my coat. You should have seen it. You could make a hundred pictures of the holes in the cotton outside. Everything was rotten. I took the coat and I just covered her up.

The day was coming soon. It was getting already light. The two boys, they would go out first from the side of the hiding place, I figured.

That's just what they did. The older one was 11 or 12. I heard them go out together. One boy called the other, "Mendle, Mendle." He wanted him to stay near him. If I called them, maybe they'd get scared and not answer me, and I'd be lost. But I decided to shout with a loud voice, a big voice. "Motle, Motle, tell me how to get there. Tell me how to get there." They were afraid that I was hollering.

"Simon, Simon, Simon," they yelled.

"Call me quietly. Call me quietly. Lead me to where you are," I said. And that's what they did.

I got there. I pushed in Sophie downstairs. And I went in after her. She couldn't lie down. She was on her knees. Fischel was lying in the corner, comfortable, spread out; he started to move, but too slowly. My head was still outside, above the ground.

"What are you doing here? What's happening?" they asked me. I didn't answer.

I pushed my hand to Fischel and I moved him. I didn't talk to him; I just moved him to where Sophie was. And I put Sophie where he was. Then I started telling them what happened.

In the daytime, we hid in this hole. It was about 4 feet high. The only place for me was in the entrance. There was no place for me to lie down, but I was happy that I had a place for Sophie.

And Fischel? He made a place for himself in a corner, but he was complaining. I told him, "You don't complain nothing." I was sitting near the hole with my feet under me and my head sticking out about 2 or 3 inches. I had a lot of hair because I didn't take haircuts. I didn't have scissors. In the winter time I was needing the hair to keep me warm.

From the people who were hiding, from their breath, it got warm and the air came outside and made a frost. The frost right away made ice. Once I woke up and felt that there was something on my head. I figured somebody was standing on my head. I touched my hair; it was full of ice. A head full of ice. I started with my hands rubbing and rubbing. And I put a piece of cloth on my head.

All of the time this was my place. I couldn't lie down. When they went out, I could lay down, and when they came back, I went back to my position. If you want to sleep, you will sleep however you are, however you're sitting. I was sitting on my feet, and sometimes my feet got numb. So I stretched.

Twice a week in the night I would go out from the hole by myself and walk to Lukasiewicz for something to eat. He didn't give me enough to last. He didn't have a lot. He gave me what he could.

I didn't tell Anton and Franka where I was hiding. I didn't tell them that we escaped from the old place. I just told them I came for some food. Why didn't I tell them? All the time there was a reason. I couldn't help it. If Anton knew it, if the Germans caught him and started beating him, he could go and bring the Germans to us. You couldn't trust anybody, even the closest brothers and sisters. We knew this. It happened before. Anton would bring me out a little bit of hot soup, and I would go back.

I tried to make certain marks so that when I came back, I could find the place. Back then, my head was working strong – today like a computer. I counted the steps to the lane. I held my head straight, because if I bent down, I would go left or right. I tried to go straight, and I counted over so many, so many, so many steps to the lane. I didn't have to mark it down because I did remember very well. Then from this lane to the main road, I counted so many steps. I stood there and I looked for certain trees. I remembered to come back to the same place.

I would find our place exactly the way I counted. We had put little trees around the place so if somebody passed by, he wouldn't see that something was there. We made it in such a way that nobody could see it. You'd have to step down to find it. I came back and I gave Sophie something to eat.

I knew that Pina and her family would go out and get something to eat. Fischel went out less often. He could go longer without food. When you are hungry for one day, you don't go. You don't have anything, but you can live. You can go one, two, three or four days without food.

In the daytime, we sat very quietly. Even when we were in the cave, we didn't talk because somebody could pass by when they were going hunting. There were wild pigs and foxes in the woods, and the Germans liked to hunt. But we knew that the Germans didn't like to go into the woods, because they were afraid of the people who might be there. So they took the local people, the Ukrainians, with them to help. Or they'd send in the Ukrainians alone to hunt and look for Jews.

If there was one German and I was alone, and I knew that he would kill me, positively, I would try the best when I can catch him to put away his gun. I would kill him, no question.

One day we heard a lot of noise in the woods. And we heard shots. We were scared to death. This went on for about 2-1/2 hours, only they weren't staying in one place. They were going, going, going; we heard that they were already far away. They didn't come near us, because when we made this cave, we made it where the bushes are so wild that nobody likes to go there. They did go around, and they didn't pass us.

Sophie ate very little. When she had a piece of bread, she would cut it into pieces – an inch or an inch and a half. She ate up one piece and she put the others on the side. An hour later, she would take another piece. I was different. When I had it, I ate it up. I could go even two days; if I didn't eat anything, I was okay. I could survive. But Sophie, when she didn't eat, she passed out plenty of times.

Once, when we didn't have anything to eat, I saw Sophie looking in my pocket. She didn't talk to me. She was looking in my pocket. Maybe I had something. This was in the daytime, and I figured at nighttime, whatever happens, I'm going. It was unbelievable what kind of weather it was. The snow was so dense, I couldn't see anything. But I'm going. I wasn't afraid. Nobody would be out in such a weather. Nobody would be out at nighttime because the Germans had a law that if they caught you out at night, they would kill you. So I went out.

When I came to the main road, I didn't take it. I crossed the road and went into the other woods. I walked the five or six miles to Anton's house. I thought maybe he would let me inside this time; I should warm up. But he told me to wait outside. He asked me why I came in such weather.

"What's the difference if I die on the way?" I told him. "If I will have nothing, how long can I be without food?" He brought me out meat, and I ate right away, and he gave me a little bit of vodka. It warmed me up a little bit.

He was afraid to let me inside. If I stayed outside, he could say somebody came here in the night and asked me for something and I gave him something. But if he let me into the house, and somebody, a neighbor, saw it, and that neighbor would tell the Germans, the Germans would kill him right away, no questions.

So, I am trying to go back, and when you're walking, the snow is so heavy, you warm yourself up. I became very warm. It took a long time because I was deep in snow. It took three hours, maybe more.

I gave Sophie a piece of bread and the children started begging me, "Simon, Simon, give me something to eat." I gave them little pieces, very little, because you couldn't do it. The others didn't ask.

What could I do, take it out from my mouth and put it into theirs? I took a risk to go, and when you are going in the nighttime, it is two ways: Either you come back or you never come back. When they catch you, you're done.

The next day, the wind started a little bit lower. The snow was falling a little lighter. Cold it was enough. They did go for something to eat, so I didn't have to.

This went on for a long, long time – a whole winter. We went to this place at the end of January, and I became free from this on March 31, 1944. I was there two months in this cave.

JACOB POTASH AND PINA POTASH AFTER THE WAR IN CANADA. THEY, TOGETHER WITH PINA'S CHILDREN, MOTLE AND MENDLE, HID IN THE WOODS WITH SIMON AND SOPHIE.

MOTLE POTASH AT AGE 15.

LEFT TO RIGHT: MOTLE (MORLEY) POTASH WITH HIS YOUNGER BROTHER MENDLE (MARTIN) IN CANADA, 2004.

Simon Sterling after the war, Germany, 1946.

9

The 40-Day Typhus

I was very strong then; I could stay in ice water. It didn't mean anything to me. I didn't even cough. Lukasiewicz would give me a piece of newspaper and a few leaves of tobacco. I kept it in my pocket until it dried up. Then I made a cigarette and I smoked it. I had no matches. The cotton from my coat was very dry, so I took a piece. I would sit with the cotton and some sharp stones and knock on the stones. Sometimes it took half an hour for me to make a fire.

But once, on the way home from a trip to Anton's, the time he gave me the news that the Russians were coming closer and closer, I didn't feel so good. I felt that there was something wrong with me. Who I should tell, I didn't know. I'm sitting at the entrance of the hole, and my hair gets frozen. I had a little hat on my head, but it fell off. I fell asleep and my hair got frozen again. I laid down and I felt that I was sick. I had a high fever. The first night that I got fever, I was saying to them some things that didn't fit. They saw that something was wrong. I was lying down, so Sophie went away from her place and sat at the entrance – but she was smarter. She put my old coat over her head and the ice didn't hit her.

There was nothing that could be done for my high temperature. I wanted water. Water. I wanted to drink water, so they took the snow and melted it in a bucket. Sophie always prepared snow. I grabbed the snow and put it in my mouth. I didn't want to eat anything, I just wanted water.

When I became sick, this was the end of my going into the woods. I didn't go out anymore, so I missed plenty of things. I missed the many things that were going on in this cave. Pina went to a farmer who helped her. The farmer's wife was a very nice woman, but he was a half crazy man. I knew him before. Pina never told this man where she was hiding. She would say, "I'm in this wood or in that wood or that place," because he was not a reliable person, although he didn't care that his wife was giving her something to eat. He told her that people in the town were organizing, that they wanted to go into all the woods to look for Jews. They were searching for the partisans. She came back and told us this story. They wanted to move, to go away.

Only me, I'm sick. I didn't even know what they were talking about. I'm not interested. I had once read in a book about Honolulu, that it was a resort of some kind. This came into my mind while I had the fever: I'm in Honolulu, sitting in a wide chair with my feet in a warm bucket of water. I'm sitting like the whole world belongs to me. And then all of a sudden my mind changed into different things. So they talked to Sophie.

"You want to go with us? We are going away," Pina said.

"How can you go away? What about Simon?" Sophie asked.

"Look, he will not be long around anyway," she answered.

Sophie refused to go. Fischel, Pina, her two boys, and Jacob went to her farmer. They hid in his barn. If he knew about it, they would be in very bad shape. They stayed there over the day, and in the night they came back.

I had typhus. There are two kinds: one is 11 days and the other is 40 days. I had the second type now. It was like inside typhus. Forty days of temperature, and it was contagious.

You only get each type of typhus once, and all the people who were with me already had it in the ghetto – and survived. But a lot of people didn't survive typhus in the ghetto. I had the 11-day typhus before.

Sophie wanted to go for food, so Fischel went out with her. He knew the way to Lukasiewicz's. He hid behind the barn while Sophie went up to the window and knocked. She told Anton and Franka that I was sick, so they gave her something to eat - some cookies that the priest had brought. The two of them went there several times that March.

There was a time when I could chew something, but then I just wanted water, water, water and water. I laid there with typhus. They saw that I was so sick and they thought today, tomorrow I would be gone. So when the snow melted a little bit, Fischel and Yossel – they didn't ask anybody – dug a hole for me, for when I would become cold feet. But I survived with my high temperature.

The Russians were approaching and the Germans were moving back, and for about two weeks we had been hearing shooting from the machine guns. But there was a lake that the Russians couldn't pass over; and they stayed on one side of it for about eight days. So the Germans came back; they were now all around. How long would we be able to survive here?

Fischel, Pina, Jacob, and the boys decided that since they could swim – we lived in a small town with a lake and everyone could swim – they would swim the lake and get to the other side where the Russians were. They could be killed by the Russians, too, only they were afraid to stay where they were.

They talked to Sophie. "Sophie, you want to go with us?"

"No. How can I go when Simon can't move? I will not leave him alone," she said. So they were thinking and thinking about going, and they finally decided not to go.

By the end of the month, March 31, there was no more shooting. It was so quiet. We were in the woods, so we didn't see anybody. We were deep inside. What was going on there we could only hear – the automobiles, the noise in the woods. We didn't know who it was. Maybe it was the Germans.

One day, when Sophie was sitting near by the entrance hole, she heard someone hollering. It was the Russian toast: "Should live the father Stalin."

I didn't hear anything. Sophie put her head out, and she recognized my brother Isak's voice. Only it was very suspicious. Maybe the Germans caught him and told him to holler to get us out. Maybe the Germans made him do that. But he didn't stop, and then he shouted in Yiddish, *"Kim aros mir zenin frei!"* ("Come out. We are free, we are free!") Fischel and Sophie went out to him.

Only I couldn't move. I was lying there. I didn't know what was going on. I still had a high temperature, and I was already thin like nothing. I don't know how I made it. No medicine, no nothing. They took me out of the cave, my brother on one side, and Fischel on the other, and they carried me. I couldn't move my feet. They took me to a farmer's house; Russian soldiers were already there. I started to understand what was going on.

Sophie told me that Isak had been hidden by a Gentile in another place far away when the Russians came. He knew where we might be, because he had helped us make the hiding place for Fischel and Pina, and he knew we would use it if we had to. He knew how to get there, only he couldn't remember exactly where the place was. So he went into the woods and started hollering.

Sophie got somebody with a horse and wagon to take me into town, into Szczurowice, where we were had been living. It was not far. They took us to our house, only a family was living there already. When they saw us, they moved their things out right away. We went in.

The next day, Sophie took me to the priest, Mazak, who was living two or three blocks from us. I couldn't walk, but she got me there. He saw how sick I was and gave me something to eat. He gave me butter, and he talked to me. I couldn't talk too much because I still had temperature. He was talking to me like this: "You will get well and you are free now." The free, that I became free, this gave me so much strength to live. I wanted to live, and this helped me.

10

Hunger And The Hospital

It was March of 1944, and the war was still going on not far from us; in the daytime they were bombing. The Russian soldiers, the officers, came to town and tried to give us things to help us. There was one Jewish officer, and he told me, "You better run away from here. Our troops may be moved back five or ten miles. If you stay here you'll be a dead person." The people in the town would kill us, and so would the Germans.

It had been about a week since we arrived back in Szczurowice, and I was already coming back to myself. We wanted to cross the river to where the Russian commando was. We would go with the Russian soldiers. My brother was already there on the other side because he could walk.

I couldn't walk, but Sophie was feeling better. The will for life was so strong; all of a sudden she became strong. She could go and the strong Simon could not move. When I was going over the bridge with her, I held myself up near the side and Sophie shouted at me, "Simon Simon, faster, faster." I should go faster. But I couldn't go faster. I got mad at her because she was hollering at me to move faster, faster, and I couldn't.

We had about two miles to go to get to the Russian commando. I felt like I couldn't really go. I was moving, but I went a little and then I sat down. We were in a line and no one cared what happened if people fell down. The Russians were moving and they just passed people by. The German airplanes were bombing us from above. I didn't care at this time; I didn't care about the German airplanes.

Sophie took me to the village were the Russians were. "Where is there a doctor?" she asked.

They found a doctor. My temperature was still high. The doctor told Sophie that if I found something to eat, I shouldn't eat it all at one time, just a little at a time. The Russians gave me a little soup.

I was there for about three or four days, and every minute I was feeling better and better. But the doctor said to Sophie, "Let him go with the soldiers who are wounded. I'll put him in with them and he will go to a hospital in Dubno. There he will get some treatment." When I asked the doctor if Sophie could go with me, he said no.

They put me into a horse and wagon with wounded soldiers. We were all lying in the wagon. It was already spring. It really wasn't so warm, but it was still very good. I remember thinking to myself, "I am free; I am free." I couldn't believe it. Sometimes I had to pinch myself to know that this was not a dream. I couldn't believe it. Nobody could have believed it.

It took us three days to travel the 80 miles to Dubno. They stopped in every village, and the farmers had to bring out milk and feed us. We stopped in towns to warm up. I was a sick man, just like the wounded soldiers.

The Russian soldiers took Sophie to Dubno in their trucks. The Russian people, they were people like every people. There was no difference between us and them. They knew what Hitler did to the Jewish people and they tried to help. They were with us. And they suffered themselves.

Sophie didn't know where the hospital was, but she found it. And she found me there, lying in bed. They gave us not too much to eat. My temperature was still high, but I was hungry. I wanted to eat, and there was nothing to eat. I went around the hospital begging: "Somebody give me something to eat."

I saw a Russian with a whole bread. He had gone out of the hospital area. He had plenty of rubles; they were nothing. He paid 40 or 50 rubles for bread from the farmers. So I told him, "Please give me a piece of bread." He didn't want to give it to me.

"You have to give me some. I'm hungry. I'm hungry," I told him. I knew the Russian language, so I told him, "When I will be wealthy, I will bring you ten breads. You give me a piece of bread."

He gave me some, and then others gave me bread. They helped me, and every minute – minute by minute – I became stronger. Still, my high temperature didn't want to go away.

In the meantime, the Germans came to Dubno and bombed the town. All the soldiers had to run downstairs to a hiding place under the building. I didn't go. I wasn't afraid of the bombs. I figured the war was coming to an end and Hitler was defeated. I didn't care about my life. There was only one thing to live for, to see that Hitler was defeated.

The Dubno hospital was filled up; the rooms were packed with five in a room. People were on the floor. What's the problem with the floor? You can sleep on the floor. You can sleep on steel if you get used to it.

They took all the sick people to the Dubno railroad station. When I got there I was feeling very weak. There was a platform made from wood, about the size of a bed, and I right away went to that platform and laid down. Some of the other people couldn't lie down by themselves; they had to be helped. I figured to myself: This is a good spot for me. This is a good place. It was hard; there was nothing on the bottom. But I could live all my life on this table; I felt so good. I didn't want anything better.

I was afraid to move; if I did someone would take my place. But at nighttime, I became very hungry. So when everybody was already lying down or asleep, I put on my coat and my shoes. Shoes I wouldn't trust to leave. My coat I didn't worry about; the cotton from the inside was on the outside, and everything was torn. I went out. There was a conductor there, and I knew somebody had some food in his pocket or somewhere.

I went to him and said, "I'm hungry. Give me something to eat."

"Who are you? You are not a soldier. Where did you come from?" he asked.

I told him I was one of the survivors – from the woods and from the camps. He made me hot tea; he made it himself in a corner so that no one would see. He put in sugar and gave me a piece of bread. When I drank the tea and ate the piece of bread, in my eyes I saw the whole world. I could see it.

He gave me tobacco and newspaper. I wrapped the tobacco with the newspaper and I smoked a cigarette. And the whole world belonged to me. I went back to my place and I felt like God. If someone had a hundred million dollars, he would not feel like I felt.

I'm lying on the hard bed, and it didn't bother me a bit. Quite the opposite.

I figured to myself, I'm a free man. I'm between the Russians. They're fighting Germany, and when I get better, right away I'm going with the Russian army to fight the Germans.

From the station I went to see the doctor at the hospital. He took my temperature and it was high – 102, 104, 103. Every day it was a little different, but it was high. Sophie was in Dubno, and she would come to me. The soldiers would make fun of me. They would say to her, "Woman? He needs a woman? Now look at him." But she didn't pay any attention to what they said.

One night, the Germans bombed Dubno very hard and many people were killed. When I went to the doctor the next morning, he told me that if I wanted to live, he would send me to a hospital in Zhitomir, deeper in Russia. When I told Sophie the news, she told the doctor that she wanted to go with me.

"You cannot go with him," he told her. "There are trains that come through here with sick people. I am putting him on a train, and he'll go to the hospital there. You cannot go there."

The next morning, they put me on a freight train. They packed in one wagon a lot of sick people; many of them couldn't walk. Before the train started to move, the Germans started bombing so hard. A lot of the sick soldiers who could move jumped off the train to hide in the fields. I didn't go anyplace, and there were a few others who didn't move. I was not afraid from the bombs. I couldn't go out easily; I was still walking with the crutches they gave me at the hospital. From the typhus I was paralyzed in one leg and in one hand. If I got off, the train might go away and I wouldn't be able to get on again. I would be left there.

When the bombing stopped, the train started on its way to Zhitomer, which is a nice little town. They took us on trucks from the train to a big hospital. It had bunk beds, three on top of each other. Each bed had a little straw. I was lying on the second bed, in the middle.

The hospital had a kitchen, but they didn't bring food to the bed. No matter how sick you were, you had to get up and go to the kitchen to get your food. I didn't trust anybody to bring me food.

They could eat up half before they came back. So I, with the crutches, went to the hospital kitchen to eat.

When the cook gave me some soup, I said to him, "Give me some more. I'm hungry." I didn't move with the crutches. I didn't move from my spot. So he gave me some more. Nobody knows what hunger means. Hunger takes away from the person all his. . . he will do everything to satisfy his hunger. In the hospital I was going around with crutches. With all my going around, I was always so hungry. I was only looking for places to find food.

I had a pair of boots. They were still good from the ankles up, but they were completely rotten at the bottom. If you put a little water from a glass, the water would go through right away. The bottoms were tied up with wire so they would stay on. A Russian soldier saw the tops of the boots. They were high boots, and the tops were still nice. He figured if he could get my tops, he could make a pair of boots by getting other leather and making the bottoms.

He told me I should change with him. He would give me a pair of shoes, and I should give him the boots.

"Yes, but I also want some money for the boots," I told him. They had money. I didn't have anything. I asked for 300 rubles and he gave it to me. I took off my boots and gave them to him, and he gave me a good pair of shoes. And I had the rubles.

No sick person could go out from the area of the hospital. Soldiers were staying there, and nobody could go out. I heard there was a bazaar in town, where the farmers brought things to eat. They also sold tobacco, which they grew by themselves. It was not fine cut; it's like you take leaves and dry them up and make tobacco for cigarettes. They measured their tobacco in glasses. Ten rubles for a glassful.

I decided to go to the bazaar. This is how I escaped: There was a wooden fence around the hospital. I went to it and with my crutch I kicked out a couple boards of wood. I walked to the bazaar with my crutches. What could they do to me? They might take me back and put me in jail. But I was not afraid.

First, I bought one bread for 40 rubles. I sat down on the ground and started to eat it. I saw that half the bread was already gone. I put the remaining half under my coat, which was tied around with string because I had no buttons. Wait a minute, I thought. Let me buy a few glasses of tobacco. Let me buy another bread. They have plenty of rubles there, the soldiers in the hospital. Maybe I could sell it.

I went back the same way I had come. I arranged the wooden fence the way it was before I left, and I walked back into the hospital area.

One of the sick people saw bread sticking out of the side of my coat, and he knew that I was coming from outside. You know the head works so hard by hungry people, the head works so hard.

"What do you have there?" he asked me.

"A bread," I told him.

"Do you want to sell it?"

"Yes, I want to sell it."

"How much?"

"Eighty rubles." It cost me 40; I'd sell it for 80. He gave me the rubles, and I went away from him on my crutches.

He saw that I took out some tobacco, that I was smoking a cigarette.

"You have some tobacco?" They're not ashamed to ask. No one was ashamed to ask. So I took out the tobacco. The pants that I was wearing were rotten, the knees were open, but I had tied the bottoms together with a piece of string, and I had put the tobacco inside.

I gave him a piece of paper, and he made a cigarette. He was so happy.

"Ah, you have something, you have some more tobacco?"

"Yes," I told him. I sold him a glass full of tobacco for 20 rubles. In a minute I had sold everything. But I left for me half a bread and some tobacco.

The next morning I returned to the bazaar. I fixed myself up with this bread. I found at the bazaar a piece of lard from a pig. They charged 100 rubles for it. I bought a piece. I cut it with a knife – raw. You can eat this raw.

I fixed myself up every day and I felt stronger and stronger. I figured that now was the time...

11

' *The Old Man* '

Sophie was still in Dubno, where she was staying with survivors. They took a house that was empty and they lived together. And I figured, now is the time I should go back in the war. To help finish Hitler.

Every day they were taking out the people who felt better and sending them back to fight. Only my temperature was going one day away, and the next day it came back. But I felt all right. I was going.

As I stood there in line, I thought to myself, let me go. The captain was the head of the hospital, and he was a Jew, but I didn't know it at the time. "What are you doing here?" he asked me.

I told him I wanted to go. I wanted to fight, to defeat Hitler. He asked me who I was, and I told him. He looked at me and he looked at me again. "You go out of this line. There is my office. Wait by my door."

In front of his office stood a soldier with a gun. I told the soldier that the captain wanted me to wait for him in front of his office. I was sitting outside. I had tobacco; I smoked. The whole world belonged to me. "I'm a free man, I'm a free man!" And my energy was "I am free." I'm not afraid that someone will kill me because I am a Jew.

The captain showed up and told the soldier that anybody who came around should wait outside. The soldier was not to let anyone in before the captain said so.

He told me to sit down and he asked me where I was from. He opened the drawer. What did he want from me? I wasn't afraid from him because at this time I wasn't afraid of anybody. No, I was a free man and I was with free people. He opened the drawer, and he wanted to make a cigarette or something. I saw lying there half a piece of bread and a nice big piece of cooked lard.

He was talking to me and I didn't answer him. I was looking there. And I'm sitting there and my body – not that I wanted to – but my body kept moving closer to the table. And I said to him, "Sir, Captain, can I?" and he said, "Yes, of course."

I didn't wait for him to take out his knife to cut a piece. I took out my own knife and I cut a piece of bread and a piece of lard. I always had a big knife by me. He was asking me questions and I just didn't answer him a word. I'm chewing good and I feel every minute that big life comes around in me. I ate it up. He told me to leave some for later. But I don't know what's going to be later. I did leave a little piece. I didn't put it back in his drawer; I put it on the side close to me. Not near him. Then I felt better.

"Captain, I was hungry. I didn't answer you what you asked me," I said. He started asking me everything. How it was in the ghettos and how it was in the camps. I had to tell him the whole story. He kept me maybe an hour and a half, and then he told me that he was a Jew. A Jew from Kiev. He went back to Kiev and he lost his whole family. He came back and no one was left.

"You did go in the line there; you want to go fight the Germans," he said. "There are plenty of Jewish dead. The world needs you."

I laughed and looked at him. The world needs me? "Who needs me?" I asked.

"The world needs people who survived; they should tell them what happened because nobody will believe it. We were deep in Russia and we didn't believe what we heard." And he told me, "Don't go there; you try to survive and try to get well. The war will be soon finished, and then you will start a new life."

He gave me a little courage. And I told him that I was hungry. I told him that I didn't eat. For two years I didn't have never enough. If I ate one day, I would not eat again until two days later. And my body was hungry. And when my stomach was full, I could throw it out to eat again. I couldn't help it. I was hungry. How much they gave me was not enough for me.

The captain told one of his soldiers to call the head of the kitchen. When he came around, the captain told him in Russian, "We have to build him up. Try to give him more." He told me that I should never come between the first ones in the line. I should try to be the last one. "I know it is hard for you to wait to be the last one, but it will be better for you," he said.

I had a little can that I tied it to my belt with a piece of wire. It was my plate. And I had a spoon, and a big knife I always had. If I got in line with this little can and put the food in, before I moved five steps I would eat it up. Then I'd be hungry again. In the trash I found a big can of food that the American government sent over – maybe a 5-pound can. I knocked two holes in it. I put in a wire, and I attached it to my belt. I threw away the little can.

I came in line with the big can. This time they had hot dogs and mashed potatoes. The head of the kitchen filled me up a full can, and it was heavy. I was afraid to go out with this, so I covered the can with my old coat. Nobody should see. In the hospital there was a little place with bushes. I sat down between these bushes and ate the hot dogs. I still feel today how this did taste. Mashed potatoes and hot dogs.

I was eating and eating and I felt, oh, oh, in a minute I'm going to throw up. So, I said, "Simon, you stop." I ate maybe half a can. So what to do? I took some leaves from the bushes (I didn't have a top for the can) and I put a lot of leaves on top. I dug out with my hands a little hole in the earth. I put the can down inside and covered it up with the leaves. I felt very good.

I walked around with the crutches and a cane. I don't know how I could walk around. One leg couldn't move, but I walked. You know what they called me at this time? In English it would be "the old man." I was 39 years old. They called me "the old man." That's how I looked, like an old man with my hair and no haircut. I started shaving once a week.

In this kitchen they fed me up and I became stronger and stronger. Then the captain told me, "I will send you now to another place, an army base. It's a place where people are working for the army. There you will be all right. It's in Russia."

I agreed. I couldn't be in the hospital any longer. I was doing better.

When I came to the army base, I found a lot of survivors like me. They had been sent from other hospitals to work, too. I was working with the Russians, and I was getting stronger.

Sophie was in Dubno with the other survivors. I knew where they were staying, and I wrote her a letter. A soldier delivered it for me, and Sophie begged him to wait a few minutes while she answered my letter. "Simon, come back here. Come back to Dubno, and we will go to Lemberg from here."

I didn't know. I was already registered. I was working in an army base and how could I get out? How could I go?

So I went to the captain and told him that my wife was there in Dubno and I wanted to bring her here. "Forget about it; you cannot go," he said.

I asked around: How could I get from him a paper?

"You want something from him, you go out and buy a couple bottles of vodka," I found out. I had already rubles, so I went and bought the vodka at the bazaar and brought it to the captain in the office. There was a glass on the table. I took it and I asked "You have another glass?"

"Yes," he answered.

"Give me another glass." I filled up half the glass with vodka for him and I poured myself the same. I took out the bottles I had with me and put them on the table. "Give me the note," I told him. He took out a pencil and wrote down that I was going to pick up my wife.

I decided to go by train (at this time there were only freight trains). But when I showed the train official my letter from the captain, he said, "This is no good. You have to go to the army headquarters; they have to give you the pass."

When I went to the army headquarters, they didn't know what I was talking about or who I was. What to do? I never did give up because if you give up, you're gone. So I looked around and there was a little man. He looked like a Jewish man. There weren't many Jewish people around. A lot escaped deep in Russia, but in this area, there weren't many around. Hitler killed them.

As I passed him by, I said, *"Amcho."* That's a Hebrew expression we used to identify ourselves to another Jewish person. And he looked at me and he asked me in Yiddish, *"Fin vanet bist du?"* ("From where are you?") I told him the story. My wife was in Dubno, and my plan was to bring her here. We should be together. After the war, we would go where we could go.

"Bist du meshugga?" ("Are you crazy?") Why do you want to go for your wife? You don't need to go for your wife. After the war you'll have plenty of wives. You don't have to go for the wife. The war is still not finished there." He was serious.

"She's there and I want to be with her. How can I get a ticket?" I asked.

"You have some rubles?"

"Yes."

"Take 200 rubles, make it in your hand like a ticket. And when you go on the train, don't go in the middle of the line; wait to be the last one," he told me. "You hold it in your hand, and when the conductor asks for this ticket, you give him the 200 rubles. Put it in his hand quickly, and go into the train." And that's how it happened.

I came to Dubno in the night. The war was still not finished. About 100 miles from Dubno the war was still going on. In Dubno no one could walk around freely. The Russians were walking around; the soldiers were all over.

I knew where Sophie would be. She was in the same house as when I had left Dubno. A Russian stopped me. I had this paper. I told him I was working there and that I'd come for my wife. "I have tobacco," I said. "Do you have any paper?"

"Yes, I have paper, but I have no tobacco." So I gave him a cigarette and I made myself one. I gave him some more tobacco. He was so happy. He escorted me to the house.

The first thing Sophie said to me was this: "You're not going back. We are going to Lopatin."

"But I'm registered there," I objected.

"Registered. . . registered, what are you afraid of now? Forget about being registered. Come with me to Lopatin. There is your brother Isak."

We went to Lopatin.

SIMON AND SOPHIE IN FÖHRENWALD, A DISPLACED PERSON'S CAMP NEAR MUNICH, GERMANY, 1948, A YEAR BEFORE THEY IMMIGRATED TO THE UNITED STATES.

12

'Simeone The Brewmaster'

When we came to Lopatin, which is about 70 miles from Lemberg, the Russians gave me a job as head of a brewery. Making beer. I didn't know anything about making beer, but I told them I had some experience.

There was nothing in the brewery. They were smart; they picked the person they thought would do the job, who would find the materials. I was needing certain materials, wheat and hops. So I went to a Russian who collected wheat from the farmers for the Russian government. Everything belonged to the government. I told him I was the head from the brewery, and he should give me a ton of barley. When I made the beer, I would give it to the cooperative.

"Nothing can be done. No," he told me. I explained that I would give him a paper to show that he lent me this barley.

"Nothing can be done," he repeated.

I went back and talked to my brother, Isak. "Try to organize a few bottles of whiskey and some kielbasa," he suggested.

I borrowed the whiskey and kielbasa from some farmers, and I brought them to that Russian man. As we were drinking and eating, I said, "I need a ton of barley."

"Okay, no problem." He took out a piece of paper and wrote me a note. I should go to the grain storage area and they would give me a ton of barley.

I also needed hops. (Or how do you call it? I think it's called yeast.) He told me I could get that at a Lemberg brewery run by the Russians. So I took a farmer with a horse and wagon and we went there. The war was still on, and they were still bombing. But this war, when I was already free, was to me a minor thing. I was not afraid.

I had presents – butter and different things to eat – for the director of the brewery, who was living there with his family. I wanted to drive right inside, but a soldier stopped me. I told him I was the director of the brewery in Lopatin, that I had papers, and I wanted to see the director. The soldier let me in and showed me to his house.

I saw a man leave the house. I didn't want him to see me before I gave him what I brought for him. So when he left, I went to the woman and I asked her, "Are you the wife of the director?"

"Yes," she said.

"I have a present for you." Everything was very scarce there, and they were very happy with it. She took it from me, and I went back to the horse and wagon to wait for the director to come home.

I ate something while I waited. I would never go away anywhere without having something in my pocket to eat. My mind was still working like that; the hunger was in me all the time.

I figured I'd let the director go first into the house. He came back home, and in about five minutes I approached. He came outside to greet me, and he was very friendly. I told him who I was, and what I wanted from him. And he said, "Yes, I have plenty of this." He gave me everything I needed. I rested there for a few hours and then we went back. To go from Lemberg to Lopatin with a horse and wagon took about a half a day and a night.

I was ready to make beer. The head of the Russians – he's the secretary, the one boss, the top, the last word – I went to him and told him that I had everything, and they gave me a chemist. The chemist already prepared everything. I didn't understand anything about beer. The chemist made it.

The beer can be good when you're starting in a big container, in the big vats. Thousands of gallons go in there. It has to ferment inside for 21 days before the beer will be good.

In six or seven days, the head of the authorities came in and asked me how it was going. I told him everything was going fine. There was a little glass window in the vat and it showed the color of the beer. It was brown. "It looks good," he said.

The chemist had told me nothing could be touched. If you opened the vat, the beer could be spoiled. This man, the head of the region here, said he wanted to try it. He asked me to open it up. "Forget about it. Forget what the chemist said," he told me. And he took a glass of beer.

"It's very good. It's very good beer." He was pleased.

He left and in about 10 minutes the phone rang. It was him. He told me he had a party that night and I should send him three barrels of beer. I told him the beer was still not ready.

"Send me three barrels of beer," he repeated.

What could I do? With him I can't argue. So we prepared three barrels and I sent them over to him. Over the 21 days, officials came to the brewery. I had to give them beer, and they drank.

In the end, we gave the beer to the cooperative and they brought us barley in return. We didn't deal in money now; everything was bartered. I gave back to the farmer the original ton of barley which he lent me, and everything was all right. But then, after the beer was finished and we had to start again to make more, we had problems. My secretary showed me in the books that I was short over a hundred barrels of beer. Short!

So I figured, I will go to this man, the head from the region, and tell him that I was short in beer and I would like him to give me a certain paper saying that he took the beer. When I told him this, he said, "You are short in beer? Then you'll go to jail."

I quickly understood that it was no use to talk to get that paper. And in the same moment my mind was working; I have to do something different. "I'm going back," I said. "Probably the bookkeeper made a mistake. I will look it over myself and recheck it."

At the door, he called to me, and he called Simeone. That's my name in Russian. "Come here." I went back to him. "Tonight we have some officials coming. We're having a big party with about 40 people. We'll need kielbasa. We'll need vodka. We'll need a lot of things that I don't have, and beer, no question."

"Everything will be here," I assured him. "What time do you want it?"

"4:30 or 5:00."

"Everything will be here," I repeated. It was about 10:00 in the morning.

I ran around. The people made vodka themselves. So I told them, "You give me vodka, and I will give you beer. Give me kielbasa, and I will give you beer." I was already something of an authority there.

They gave me what I wanted and I organized everything. I took a horse and wagon myself and I went to where this official was living. I gave him everything, and he said, "Oh, you. You're okay, you know." I knew what he meant.

When I got back to my office, I called in the secretary and the chemist. I was acting like them, like the officials. "From today on, any notes that we are putting in the book about wheat, or about amounts of beer that we make, will not be recorded unless I am here in the office. No one is to write in these books without me here," I ordered.

And they said, "*Khorosho*. Of course, you are the boss."

So came the day when I had to write in the books. The secretary started to tell me that grain, we are using so much, and beer, we will have so much.

"Grain, we didn't have so much grain; we had half the amount," I answered her. "You didn't use so much; you used half of that. Everything that you used, just half, and beer we will have half." I'm talking already stronger to them. And they were afraid of me. What I said they wrote down.

Meantime, officials were coming all the time and drinking the beer. But I was responsible. If they caught me, all these people would be against me. No matter that I gave them, they would turn against me. It was a very dangerous thing to be here.

So I went back to the Russian in charge of the area and I told him, "This is a job which is very hard for me, and I would like you should send me to Lemberg." Lemberg was the big city close from my parent's town. It was under Russian control. I made him a proposition that I would work in the cooperative in Lemberg to help distribute merchandise. When people came from that area for different things, I would make sure that they got what they needed. He thought it was a good idea.

"You want to go to Lemberg?" he asked.

"Yes. But I want to go with my wife."

Everything that I asked, he said, "Yes." So I figured, very good.

I started getting up from the chair. "Sit," he ordered. And he gave me a pencil with a piece of paper. "Mark it down." He tells me, "I'm going to visit my wife; she lives in Kiev. I cannot go empty-handed. I need a leather coat for her. I need this, I need this, I need this, I need this." He told me which store to go to.

"I'll try to organize everything," I assured him.

It took me a week, maybe more, before I went to Lemberg to find a leather coat. He gave me the measurements. He gave me a dress of his wife's that he had bought, so I could match up the size. He told me to put the dress on somebody and put the coat over that.

I bought a leather coat. I bought boots. I bought shoes and dresses. What did I do? I gave away the beer.

I had everything, and I took it to him. He went to see his wife for two or three days. When he came back, he appointed another man to head the brewery. Then, he gave me the paper I needed.

I was off to Lemberg.

SOPHIE STERLING

SIMON STERLING

THESE PICTURES WERE TAKEN RIGHT AFTER THE WAR TO BE USED AS IDENTITY PHOTOGRAPHS.

SIMON STERLING AFTER THE WAR IN GERMANY, 1946.

13

'Ani Greek!'

When we arrived in Lemberg, I went to the police. I told them who I was and that I needed a place to live. There were plenty of empty houses and apartments there. They had taken away the Jewish people, so there were plenty of apartments.

"You don't have to come to us," they said. "Just go into an apartment that you like." I looked around and I found an apartment and a little furniture that I liked.

I went to work at the cooperative, where they had merchandise to give out. They had maybe four dresses for 40 stores in 40 villages. So I took the four dresses. I was like the distributor. I had to take these to Lemberg and there they would distribute them.

I went to the other cooperatives also. Anything they had they gave to me, but they had very little. Once I got four men's fur hats. I looked at the fur and saw that they were very good fur hats, so one I put away for myself.

When the officials came to Lemberg, they would stop by where I was. They already knew about me. These guys were like from the secret police; they were just not regular officials. Once when they came around, one of the big shots walked up to me and said, "Ah, Simeone, Simeone, let's drink a bottle of whiskey." He brought out a bottle, and I had bread, so we drank and ate. He walked over to some boxes and told me, "Simeone, I have a girlfriend in Lemberg. I'm going to visit her, and I can't go empty-handed. I need a dress. What can you do for me?"

I told him I had just four dresses and I had to distribute them.

"Give them only three," he said, and he took out a dress.

I didn't send the merchandise. I didn't have enough.

Another time, a man from the secret police came in and saw the fur hats. It was winter and very cold. He said, "Oh, Simeone. I will take this hat; this is for me. What you have to do is your problem. I'm taking the hat. And you don't tell anybody that I took it."

Go tell him no. What could I do? I'm short a dress, and I'm short a hat.

So I went to the bazaar, which was like a black market. I had a good dress, and Sophie put it on over her dress and went with me. A woman there saw the dress and asked if I wanted to sell it. I told her the price in rubles – we were dealing in rubles. I don't remember if it was 300 or 400 rubles. I sold the dress to her. Others at the bazaar were selling cheap dresses for 50 rubles, so I bought four dresses for the same money. I sold one of my hats, a very good hat, and bought three others for it.

I was covered. All the time I had to cover what they were taking away from me.

I was working in Lemberg for a few months; it was the beginning of 1945. The war was still going on, though it was near the end.

At this time in Lemberg, the biggest percentage of people were Ukrainians; only about 20 percent were Poles. Just a few Jewish people were left, because in Lemberg, and in the area around it, there were no concentration camps – only death camps. And in the Ukraine, Dubno, Lutsk, there were no concentration camps. There was liquidation. Liquidation. They liquidated the Jewish people in these places. So there were very few left. There were survivors like me, who had been hiding in the woods. Others couldn't take it; it was not so easy in the woods. It is very hard to explain to somebody.

When the war ended, the Russians gave an order to all the Polish people in the area to move out. Lemberg would become Ukrainian territory. Some farmers left with their horses and wagons. They went deep into Poland and they settled in Silezia. The German people who had been living in Silezia were sent back to Germany.

The remaining Jews could do the same thing as the Poles – no other groups, only the Jews who survived and the Poles.

I figured this was our chance to get away from here, to get away from the Russians, to go to Poland. Maybe from Poland there would be a chance for us to go overseas: to Israel or the United States. I gave up the job there in Russia. I told them I was going to Poland. They said all right, and another man took over my position.

So we, and the few other Jewish people left in Lemberg, found somebody with a truck and left for Poland. We came to Cracow, where we all took one apartment together. Our hope was only to go away from Poland, from Russia. . .

At this time, Poland was controlled by the Polish people under Russian rules. Under Communist rule. There were plenty of Russians around, but the Poles controlled what was going on day by day. And they wouldn't let anybody go out from Poland.

But I went around and I heard things. I saw by the train, into the city, came people from the war, prisoners from the camps – from Greece, from Czechoslovakia, from Hungary. The Russians let them come to Poland.

The group of us in the apartments decided we would make ourselves Greek. Why would we pretend to be Greeks? Because the Poles didn't understand the Greek language, and when we came to the border, they wouldn't know that we weren't speaking Greek.

We had to go to the Polish border and then through Czechoslovakia. From there, we were supposedly going to Greece. We got caps like the Greeks wore. We didn't have anything to pack, so we packed a little bag, mostly filled with food. Without food, I don't walk one mile. The hunger was for so many years that in my mind I should always have something to eat with me.

The war was finished and we figured we'd try to cross at the closest border first. If they didn't let us, we would have to walk 15 miles in another direction to cross the border over some water. That was our plan.

When we got to the border, the Russian soldiers asked us where we were going. They tried to speak to us in Polish and we pretended not to understand anything they said. They asked us where we were going again. "Ani Greek. Ani Greek!" I said in Hebrew. "I am Greek!"

"I don't see that these are Greeks," one soldier said.

"What do you care who they are? What's the difference to you? Let them go," said the other.

"Greek, Greek, Greek," we kept telling them.

Finally, the other agreed. "Go," he said. So we went. By foot we passed over the border into Czechoslovakia.

We didn't want to be there.

On our journey, we found out that the Americans were in Munich. We heard the news from some Polish people who returned to Poland from Germany. We asked them how was it there. "Oh, the Americans treated us wonderfully," they reported. "The Americans gave us food and cigarettes and they took care. There's nothing better than the Americans." So, we figured, let's go to the American Zone.

We came to a town with a train station. We didn't need any money; nobody was asking for tickets. The only ones who were traveling were from other countries trying to reach other places. We asked which train was going to the German border. Even the conductors didn't know where the trains were going.

Finally there came a train that was going in the right direction. It was packed with Russian soldiers with prisoners of the war. We jumped in – actually, we pushed ourselves in. First, Sophie. I was already stronger, so her I pushed into a window. The train started moving, and people were on the roof. I held onto the train with my hands. It wasn't going a hundred miles an hour; it was going like a horse and wagon. While it was moving, I pushed myself in.

At the German border everybody had to get off the train. It didn't go any farther. On our side at the border was only the Russian army. "Ani Greek," we said. "We're going to Germany, and from Germany we're going to Greece."

They didn't ask further. They let us go over the border.

We were going to walk to a village about five miles into Germany. As soon as we crossed, there were already American soldiers on the other side – nicely dressed. They started talking to us, but we didn't understand anything. I said, "Greek, Greek. Ani Greek."

We were with a group of 100 or so people, all coming from Czechoslovakia. About three or four soldiers took us with them. One soldier had a whole pack of cigarettes. He took one for himself and gave the rest to everybody. We were feeling very free.

They took us into a camp with big buildings. In the camp was the American army. We were afraid from them, too, because if they didn't like something, they could send us back. That's what we thought. I was the first one in the group. I and another man, we represented the group. I said, "Greek, Greek. We're Greek."

The soldiers went away and returned with bread and kielbasas and soda and coffee. There were big tables. We were eating. When did we see this? And we were so happy, happy; we were like doped up in ourselves.

In came one officer and he started talking in English. "Greek, Greek, Ani Greek. We're Greeks," I repeated. We were afraid from them, too. And he said in Yiddish, "Are there any Jews here? Can we speak Yiddish to anyone here?" He knew that this Greek was a fake. He added in Yiddish, "If you are Jews, you have nothing to be afraid of. You only have to tell us that you're Jews."

"You don't have to be afraid," he continued. "I am a Jew, and we had some Jewish people like you here before. We will take care of you, and don't be afraid. Don't be afraid to tell who you are."

So I told them. "Yes, we are Jewish; we are Jewish people."

FAR LEFT: SIMON WITH A GROUP OF SURVIVOR FRIENDS IN GERMANY, 1948.

SIMON STERLING IN A DEMONSTRATION WITH HOLOCAUST SURVIVORS MARCHING
NEAR MUNICH, GERMANY IN SUPPORT OF ISRAEL'S STATEHOOD, 1948.

14

Life In Föhrenwald

"We will send you with a train. We will send you to Munich," the American officer reassured us in Yiddish. "In Munich, it is already organized for the people who survived, and you don't have to be afraid from anybody. Everything will be all right. The authority – the American Authority – is there in Munich. No German will take care of you, only the Americans. You belong under the American army."

The young boys in our group were already singing and dancing. We slept there over the night. It was like in heaven. The next day another group of 100 people arrived. They came the same way we did. They said they were Greeks. So I told them, "Don't be a Greek. You're a Jew. Don't forget it. You have nothing to be afraid of here."

The Americans organized a freight train to take us to Munich. In the meantime, they gave us plenty of food for the road. When we stopped at certain stations on the way, I got off. I figured the train would not run away, and if I didn't catch my car, I could jump into another car.

About five or six miles before Munich, they separated our compartments. The rest of the train continued on its way, and we were left there. Nobody told us for what reason this happened, but we were not afraid, because the American army was everywhere.

It didn't take more than a half hour, and along came a closed army truck with packages of food – chocolate and cigarettes and breads and different kinds of canned foods, like tuna fish. Three or four soldiers were on the truck, and there was a Jewish captain, too. "We brought you food to eat. Don't be afraid," he told us in Yiddish. He instructed us to stay in line.

When they opened the truck, our people – they were shocked from what had happened, shocked that they were alive – jumped inside. The soldiers inside the truck pushed them out. "There's plenty for everybody," the captain assured us.

I didn't do that. I didn't go in.

A lot of people took two or three times their share, and some didn't get anything. "Wait a minute," we said. "How many did you take? He doesn't have it, and she doesn't have it." So we divided it up. Everybody would have one package. We did this among ourselves, because at this point the captain had nothing to say. We told each other, "If something is left, you can have two. But if you have two and someone has none, you have to give it to him." That's what we did.

We went out into the fields. We were so happy. It was unbelievable that we were free. We were free in the daytime. We were not afraid of killing, of shooting.

The captain announced that the train would pick us up in an hour or two and take us to Munich. From there we should go to the Deutsche Museum – the German Museum. We didn't know where it was, but we heard, "Be at the German Museum."

At the Munich train station, we were told to go to the autobahn, which is like a trolley car. When we boarded, we found some German people on it. We shouted at them, *"Heraus, Heraus!"* ("Out, Out!") just like the Germans used to shout at us. And they all went out. When they saw us, they ran from us. They were afraid from us.

We packed into the trolley and told the conductor to go to the Deutsche Museum. He was afraid himself; he was shivering. We were not afraid. You didn't see a German person. You didn't see a German policeman with a gun. We were under American protection. Everything there was American.

We found a lot of people already at the museum. It was a tremendous big place, and thousands and thousands of people could go in there. Everything was organized by the American army. There were kitchens and food. Most important was the food, not only for me but for everybody. Everybody's mind was on food. When you get hungry one day, you eat up and you forget that you were ever hungry. But if you are hungry for years, it's different. I didn't have a piece of sugar for years. I didn't know what it was for years. Just a potato, a raw potato, a carrot and a piece of bread. It could have been stale bread. You couldn't bite into it, so you would have to put it in water.

Even this was good.

They divided all the displaced persons into groups so they could take us to different camps. These camps had belonged to the German soldiers, but they were now gone. I personally wanted to stay in Munich, but Sophie said we should go with the other people to the camps. I already had found some people in Munich who I knew, and they had told me, "Simon, stay in Munich. Why do you have to go there? Munich is a town; it's a city."

I went to the camp because I didn't want to fight with Sophie.

They took us to a camp called Föhrenwald, where they gave us a room. Everything was supplied by the Americans. The trucks came from the American army. They organized a kitchen where we went for breakfast, lunch and supper. They gave us plenty to eat, and they gave us shirts and boots and other clothes.

At Föhrenwald they made me a kind of a judge. There were some thefts and other problems in the camp, and they needed people to take care of it. They chose from the survivors three people: someone who was like a judge before, someone who was a lawyer, and me. We listened to people and decided what to do. I was the easiest of them all. I always told them, "Try to look at it through his eyes. Try to see what he did with his thoughts and reasons." I always wanted to let them go. If I had an education, I would be a lawyer today. I think I would be a good lawyer.

Though we stayed in Föhrenwald, we could go wherever we wanted. It took me a long time: I didn't believe that I was a free person. A free person! I couldn't believe it myself. I wanted to go to Munich because I was free. And we didn't need any money to go. The trains and everything were free for us.

My brother Isak was in Munich. He was himself alone. He had had a wife and two children, a boy of 17 and a girl of 12. They had all been killed.

We knew that we had family in the United States – in Philadelphia. I remembered that my mother's family's name was Bodek, but we didn't have an address. We didn't know how to contact them. Everybody was trying to write to family in the United States or Canada. Some wanted to go to Israel. We didn't know exactly where we wanted to go, but we hadn't come to Germany to stay in Germany.

We went to the American army headquarters in Munich and asked who understood the Jewish language. There were plenty from the army who were Jewish, but only a small number could speak Yiddish. Theirs was a very broken Yiddish, but they could understand.

A lieutenant, who was about 30 or 40 years old, understood Yiddish. He got a Philadelphia telephone book and looked up Bodek. He found a few people by that name. He mentioned the names, different names, American names. I did remember Wolfe Bodek and Aaron Bodek. They were no longer alive. There were three or four others named Bodek.

"I will make a letter to all the Bodeks that we find here. You will tell me how you are related to them. If this is the right Bodek, they will give you an answer. Okay?" the lieutenant offered.

I told him that my mother was a Bodek; she had there in Philadelphia three brothers: Wolfe, Aaron and Beryl. They had moved from Szczurowice to the United States before I was born, but I do remember because my mother was always mentioning their names. When he was 75, my grandfather, Moshe Bodek, went to visit them in Philadelphia. He spent a year there. The lieutenant wrote this in the letter, too, and mailed the letters to the United States.

We received a letter from Paula Ellis, my first cousin. Her father and my mother were brother and sister. Her letter was in English, and we found an American to interpret it for us. Paula knew exactly who we were, so she answered our letter. She wrote that they would do the best they could to bring us to the United States. We were very happy about this.

We also found a first cousin in Hartford, Conn., with the name of Sam Gross. His mother and my father were sister and brother. We wrote a letter to Sam Gross and received an answer from him, too.

Paula sent us some packages from the United States. We wrote to Paula and her family all the time. They wrote to us that they applied. We should go to the United States. Only at this time the law in the United States didn't let anybody in. So we waited.

Then Paula wrote that a friend of the family, Judge Louis Leventhal, was in Frankfurt, Germany, working with General Clay.

He was there to represent the Jewish people in the displaced persons camps. He was a big officer there; when he was traveling with a car, he had chauffeurs and guards all around him. Along with her letter, Paula had sent a photograph of the judge. Before he left for Germany, he had made a party and invited Paula; this photograph was on the reverse side of the party invitation.

We decided that my brother, Isak, and I should go visit him. General Clay's headquarters was a tremendous big building. Soldiers were all around. You couldn't go near it for 20 blocks. The street was closed up; nobody could ride there; nobody could walk there.

We came there and the soldiers asked us in English where we were going. We were already strong by this time. We didn't understand English, but we did understand Yiddish, German, Polish and Russian. So they sent us a soldier who understood German. We spoke German very good this time. We told him we had an invitation to see Judge Leventhal, and I showed him the photograph.

"Yes, this is Judge Leventhal," he said. He sent us to the next guard, and we told him the same thing. "Go further, go further and then you will come into the building," he told us.

We went into an office, and there were a lot of foreign people – from military and civil high authorities. The soldier told us to sit down and wait.

When it was our turn, we walked up to the man at the desk. *"Sprechen sie Deutsch?"* ("Do you speak German?") I asked him.

"Yes," he answered.

I told him we had an invitation to Judge Leventhal. He looked at the picture. "This is not an invitation," he said.

"If you don't want to believe this, call him up," I said. The judge knew that we were coming to see him because Paula had written him a letter. The guard didn't want to call him. He told two soldiers with guns to lead us to the building where Judge Leventhal was. It was the same place where General Clay worked.

We weren't afraid, even to be put in jail. They would give us food to eat; they would not beat us; they would not do anything to us.

We took an elevator up to the judge's office. In the front room there were about 20 officers, each sitting at a table doing work. I didn't know Judge Leventhal's face, but I saw from the picture that he was not in this first office. The soldiers who escorted us announced that they had two people who had an invitation to see Judge Leventhal. He asked for our names, looked at the invitation and opened up his book. He saw that we didn't have an appointment with the judge. When I saw him looking in his book, I thought to myself, "Oh, no; they're going to take us down to jail now. They have to investigate who are these people."

Let me try something, I figured. So I said to him, *"Farshtais Yiddish?"* ("Do you understand Yiddish?").

"Yes," he answered.

I spoke to him in Yiddish. "You send the other soldiers out, and then I'll tell you right away who I am. Make sure the soldiers don't take us down again."

He looked at us. He was a Jew, too, so he told his two soldiers to leave. I told him who I was. I told him my family was from Philadelphia and Judge Leventhal was related to my family. He rang the bell and told the judge that people with the names Simon and Isak Sterling claimed that so and so. . .

"All right, let them in. Let them into my office," the judge agreed.

This man led us to his office. As we entered, Judge Leventhal told him something quietly, which I later found out was not to interrupt us, not to allow anyone to come in. When we were finished, we would come out.

In the office, guarding the door, was a soldier with a gun.

Judge Leventhal sat in a big chair behind a large desk. It was a desk like a judge would sit in; it was so high. He told us to sit in the two chairs in front of him. He looked at us and looked at us, for maybe 10 minutes. He didn't open his mouth. He just looked at us. I didn't care. I don't mean I didn't care; I mean that I wasn't afraid. You know, I'm always mentioning afraid, because always I was afraid – for so many years. Now I'm not afraid.

"First I want to ask you one thing. You tell me how you came here," he said in Yiddish. So we told him the whole story: how we had gotten his photo from Paula Ellis and how we got through to see him – without an invitation.

First he told us about the family. "You have a very nice family in Philadelphia: very good people, charitable people, nice family. You don't have to worry too much and you will go to the United States. "I'll do what I can so you can go to the United States as soon as possible," he told us. "How much family do you have here?"

I told him I had a wife, my brother, and my wife's brother, Michael.

"I don't want to ask you too much what you went through. I know everything; I'm sitting here and I know the whole story, exactly what happened." He held us in his office maybe three-quarters of an hour, and nobody interrupted us.

"Maybe you need something?" he asked. "I can arrange that you have everything you need." I told him we were in Föhrenwald and there the food was very good. We had there the kitchen.

His wife was in Germany also, only she didn't work in his office. She was in uniform, too – an American uniform. One day she came to visit us in Föhrenwald; she brought us a nice package.

We waited to come to the United States for three years. During this time, in 1946, Sophie and I had a daughter who we named Faige in memory of my mother. We changed it to Phyllis here.

In the United States Congress, there was a lot of debate about how to change the law – to make it more open – to let people come in. When President Truman came into office, he allowed more people from displaced persons camps to come in. The first to come would be people who had some family in the United States. Sophie, Michael and I got our papers, but for some reason, Isak's hadn't arrived yet. We prepared to leave, and he expected to come later.

Paula wanted to send us money, but Sam Gross told her that he had already done it. Turns out, when they made the law, they made it so that the displaced persons shouldn't have to pay for their fare. The U.S. government would pay for the trip. So, Sam Gross sent the money, but they sent it back.

SOPHIE AND HER DAUGHTER PHYLLIS IN FÖHRENWALD,
A DISPLACED PERSONS CAMP, GERMANY, 1946.

SOPHIE AND PHYLLIS IN THE DISPLACED PERSON'S CAMP, GERMANY 1946.

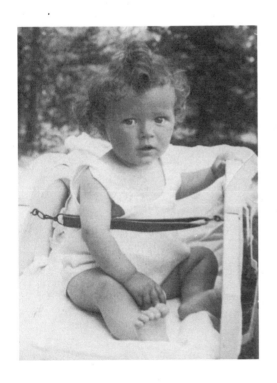

SOPHIE HOLDING PHYLLIS (LEFT), AND HER BROTHER MICHAEL'S DAUGHTER BETTY IN THE DISPLACED PERSON'S CAMP, 1946.

PHYLLIS STERLING, 1946

LEFT TO RIGHT: SIMON'S BROTHER ISAK STERLING, SOPHIE, PHYLLIS AND
SIMON IN FÖHRENWALD DISPLACED PERSON'S CAMP, 1948.

SOPHIE WITH HER BROTHER
MICHAEL REISS (RICE)
IN PHILADELPHIA, 1954.

SOPHIE AND PHYLLIS IN 1948,
A YEAR BEFORE THEY IMMIGRATED
TO THE UNITED STATES.

Simon Sterling (second from right) with survivor friends in Germany, 1948.

Simon Sterling (standing in back) with survivor friends in Föhrenwald displaced person's camp, Germany 1948.

SIMON IS STANDING (FAR LEFT) AT A WEDDING IN THE DISPLACED PERSON'S CAMP.
WEDDINGS AND BIRTHS WERE A COMMON OCCURRENCE.

SIMON IN GERMANY, 1948.

15

The Land of Promise

When we came into New York, we heard them call our name –
Sterling – over the loud speaker. They told me there was a cousin
from Hartford, Connecticut, waiting for us. Sam Gross spoke a very
basic Yiddish. He told us that he was taking us to Hartford because
Paula and Morris were in Florida. When they got home to
Philadelphia, we could decide where we wanted to live. Hartford?
Philadelphia? It didn't matter to me.

We had a good time with Sam. He was a very wealthy man. He
had a beautiful house with a beautiful garden, and he owned an
apartment house, a highrise, in Hartford. I went with him everywhere
he went. He took me to his building and we went downstairs into the
basement. He had a Jewish man working for him, a carpenter or
something.

"This is my cousin just came from Europe," Sam told the man.

And the man came up to me, tapped me on the back and
whispered Yiddish in my ear, "When Sam Gross is your cousin, you
have nothing to worry about."

When he touched me on the shoulder, he woke me up. How did
he wake me up? I figured, Sam Gross, he is a rich man, but he cannot
make me rich. He can give me $1,000, or he can give me $2,000
dollars, but I have to try to make a living myself.

This was in my mind when he tapped me on the back: "Don't
depend on someone. Depend on yourself. You survived. Try to use
your strength, so you don't have to rely on anyone."

When Paula and Morris returned home, they called Sam and
asked him to send us to Philadelphia. "If you want to stay in
Hartford, I will arrange an apartment for you. If you go to
Philadelphia and you don't like it there, Hartford is always open," he

told us. I'll never forget this.

We did go to Philadelphia. They sent us on a train. And waiting for us were Morris and Paula Ellis and their children; Paula's sister, Adel Cherry, and Adel's husband, Nathan. They took us in a car and they brought us to Paula's house.

Morris and Paula had a big house on 52nd Street with maybe 15 rooms. They had already prepared a furnished room for us. There were two women working in the house; one cleaning, one cooking. They had parties, and they introduced us to a lot of people. Some understood a little bit of Yiddish and some did not. I got along with them.

We lived in Morris and Paula's house for about four weeks. At this time, it was very hard to find an apartment, but they got us one by Seller's store, a butter and egg store in Wynnefield. They wanted us to be close to them. We were connected with Morris and with the family all of the time. They came to our apartment; we went to them.

Morris was a very fine, good gentleman. Wherever he went, I went with him. He went to business in town; I went to town. He drove me around and showed me the different places in Philadelphia. "Simon," he told me, "I was never in the retail business. I don't know too much about it." He told me that he couldn't give me any advice about the retail business.

I didn't talk because I didn't know what to say. Since I didn't know anything about the system in the United States, I figured the best policy for me would be to just be quiet and listen.

"You will work in my place," Morris told me. "And you should learn a little bit of the language." He had factories in Hagerstown, Maryland, and in Philadelphia, at 420 Market Street. He manufactured women's stockings. He made me a shipper; I packed the cartons.

Most of our New York customers spoke Yiddish. So I asked them, "How is it in New York?" They told me in New York you couldn't get lost with the Jewish language, because there were a lot of Jewish people, and most of them spoke Yiddish.

And my mind was working: How I should go for myself? How should I start it? I was always in business. In Szczurowice we had a flourmill and a lumber business. One New Yorker told me that if I went into business myself, I should stop in. He gave me his address.

After four weeks I decided I had to try it on my own. I could buy some merchandise and go to New York. I knew which styles were hot, which numbers people were looking for. I knew what merchandise was lying around. I told Morris what I was planning.

"No, no. It's too early," he said. "You still don't know the language. You still don't know too much about things here."

"It will be a long time before I learn," I told him. "I can't wait so long. I have to learn in the hard time, in the hard way."

He went home and told the family. The phone didn't stop ringing. "Simon, what's the matter? If you need something we can help you," they said. They insisted that I stay working for them. If I needed money, they would give it to me. I was scared a little bit. I didn't feel so good because I went against the family.

I told them I appreciated everything they were doing for me, but I had to try – as soon as possible. I had a wife and a child. I had made up my mind. I was going to do what I could do. I couldn't stand to be under a roof. When I was doing the shipping, I was inside. I had to be outside. This is my nature, because for the last years I was living under the sky. And here I was under a building.

One day Jack, the manager, invited me to lunch. He spoke a little Yiddish. At lunch a boy asked Jack a question. "What does he want?" I asked Jack in Yiddish. He told me the boy was looking for a job. He was still in school, but it was summertime. So I said to the boy, "Come with me. You have a job." It was my job that I was offering him. Jack looked at me in surprise.

"Jack, I'm going away," I explained. "I can't work here anymore. I have to go on my own. I have to try. I lost plenty of time in my life and I cannot lose more time. I have to do it now, right away."

"Take the boy with you upstairs. I'll go tell Morris that you found a boy to work and you will not come back to work tomorrow." Morris ran out of the office. "Simon, come in."

"I have to go do for myself, and don't worry, you will never have trouble from me," I said. "I'm not a troublemaker. You will see what I will do. I have confidence in me that I will do something and you will be proud of me."

So he didn't have any choice.

When I got back to the office, I saw that a truck had come from Hagerstown with merchandise – 100 dozen Cantron. This was women's hosiery. It was such a hot number. Everyone who came in wanted it. They couldn't make it fast enough; they didn't have the machinery.

I told Jack I wanted to buy the 100 dozen Cantron. His secretary, Roslyn, who filled the orders, was worried. "I have so many customers; I promised so many people," she said.

Morris overheard their conversation and asked what was going on. When Jack told him about the problem, Morris said, "It doesn't matter about your customers. Give it to Simon. No question."

Should I take the train to New York now or go tomorrow? I had it in my mind to go right away. I called Sophie to tell her.

"Simon, maybe it's too early," she said.

"Sophie, please don't tell me anything."

"You do what you feel to do, what you understand to do, Simon. I'm not mixing into you," she said.

While I was standing on the pavement outside Morris's factory, a New Yorker came by. He knew me because I had packed some merchandise for him. Right away he asked me, "Do you know if they have Cantron?"

"I cannot tell you if they have it. I can just tell you I'm not working there anymore. I'm in business for myself and I have 100 dozen Cantron," I answered. He looked me; he didn't answer me a word. He walked to the elevator and went upstairs. I figured he would come back because I knew there was nothing inside.

In a minute he was downstairs, "Simon, how much?"

"Listen, now you should know it. I will tell you the truth. This is the first 100 dozen that I bought, and this is my first business," I said. Morris had told Roslyn the price, and she charged me $50 less. Thirty-five years ago, $50 was a lot of money. I told him exactly the truth: how much it cost me. He gave me the full price and I made $75 profit on the deal. I had been earning $35 a week as a shipper. And at that time, $35 a week was a good salary.

He instructed me to pack up two cartons and take them to the bus station. "You wait there, and I will come," he said.

I was afraid. I didn't want anyone to steal the cartons, so I put the cartons together and I laid on them. People were going by and looking at me. What did I care that they're looking? I didn't steal from anybody. Let them look.

When he came, about an hour later, he had me put the cartons on the bus. "Now come with me to lunch," he said. At the luncheonette, he ordered for me and for him – a sandwich and coffee – and he told me, "I see that you are a person who understands business. And you will do it all right. I see it. I have confidence in you. Do you have a pencil?" he asked. "Write this down."

He gave me the numbers of the merchandise that he wanted. First, the numbers for Cantron. "How much doesn't matter; don't ask about price. If they have it, buy it. And buy me this number, and this number and this number. Anything that you will overpay, you will not lose money. You will have profit. Don't worry about profit."

And he asked me, "Maybe you need some money?" This time I had money, my own money.

"This is my address to New York," he said. "You can do the same thing next time. Take it to the bus; put it on the bus. Then, take a taxi to my store in New York."

I listened very carefully. My head was sharp. Any word he said, I remembered. I marked it down. I said goodbye to him and the bus left. I headed back into town.

Simon and Sophie with Paula Ellis in 1972.

Morris and Paula Ellis, Simon's cousins who sponsored the admission of Simon, Sophie, and Phyllis to the United States in 1949, and welcomed them warmly as family.

Left to Right: Simon, his sister Nechama Perel, who was visiting from Israel, Frank Sussman, and Sophie standing in Frank's store in Philadelphia, 1970.

16

'I Could Buy The Empire State Building'

Sometimes Morris would invite me to eat lunch with him. We would go to Horn & Hardart's at 4th and Market; all the hosiery people went there. Everybody stuck to Morris for information. I was sitting like a dummy hearing what they were talking about. They were talking in English, and I only caught some words.

Sometimes I would go to lunch there by myself. I talked to the hosiery people in Yiddish. Where is your place?" I'd ask them.

"Fourth and Market."

"And your place?"

"There on Third and Market."

All the manufacturers were around Market Street. I had their addresses. I went to them. I didn't go to Morris again. If I went to Morris, he would give me. I wanted to make it on my own. I wanted to buy it and pay for it. This was my important thing.

I came around to one man and told him, "Listen, I am in business for myself." He was in the mind that Morris threw me out. I told him I wasn't thrown out, that I wanted to go in business for myself. In fact, Morris had told me, "Try a day or two and if it doesn't work out, come back."

I bought some merchandise from this man. He packed the cartons and I took them on a hand truck to my cousin, Frank Sussman. I asked Frank if I could store cartons in his attic. He had a store on Third Street, near Market.

"Sure, bring it in," Frank said.

I went to another factory and bought a nice bunch of hosiery. I woke up early the next morning and took the cartons to the bus; the labels I already had made. In New York, I paid a taxi driver an extra 50 cents to tie the cartons to his roof, and I headed to Orchard

Street. I put the cartons in front of the door and hollered for the man. He came out and just stared at me. He couldn't understand that just a day ago he talked to me, and here I was.

He checked the order and paid me for it all. I made a nice profit – and got back to Philadelphia by 2:30 in the afternoon. It was enough time to do something else. I didn't go home. I went right into town. At home I couldn't make a living. I went to visit Morris and I told him what I did. Everything I did, I told Morris about it. He was very happy for me.

The New Yorker told me that I could ship him the merchandise by rail from the post office and he would mail me a check right away. Soon, everybody at the post office knew me. I didn't need many words; the labels were already made up. But I did begin to understand slowly, and I had a few words. I found a Polish man who worked at the post office, and I spoke to him in Polish. I found a Russian man, and I spoke to him in Russian. Someone else spoke German, so I spoke to him also. At this time, I was fluent in about five languages. I could always find someone to talk to.

On one trip to New York, I made a deal with three Jewish brothers who were in the hosiery business; they were exporting to Europe and other countries and buying big quantities. Their first order was for 2,000 dozen, in gray goods, not finished goods. Gray goods are undyed. Morris filled the order.

"When the hosiery comes, I want you to pay in 10 days," I told them.

"We're usually paying in 30 days."

"I know that," I tell him, "but pay in 10 days and then I will come back and we will do more business." They agreed.

Well, comes the ninth day and I didn't know what would happen. So I decided to go to New York; I'd stay overnight. I figured they had to pay me tomorrow.

Whenever I take an address from someone, I take it from their business and their home and from a relative. If they're not around, I can call someone and find out where they are. So I had their home address.

I got to New York and waited until night. Around 9:00, I went to the home of one brother and knocked on the door.

"Who's there?" he called out.

"Simon Sterling."

"What are you doing here?"

I was bumbling and bumbling; it was a lie and I hate to say lies. "I'm in New York and I have to stay overnight and I didn't know where to sleep. So I came to you."

"Oh, come in." In Yiddish he said, "Simon, you thief you. You didn't come to sleep over; you came for the money."

I admitted it. He understood my position. I slept over and in the morning he took me to the store. They gave me the check and an order for another 2,000 dozen.

When I came back to Morris with the first check and told him about the new order, he gave me $100. So I got $50 from the brothers and $100 from Morris. That's a lot of money. I could buy for this money the Empire State Building. That's how I felt in the beginning. Everything was very good.

It went on for about a year this way. I made some money and I put some away in the bank. I felt like I was a big shot.

Frank Sussman's store on Third Street, this was my headquarters. I had my merchandise in the attic. Frank was my cousin. When there would be a delivery of 30 cartons right in front of Frank's store, Frank would holler, "Simon, you're closing me up the door. People can't get in."

I told him, "Frank, I thank you very much for taking me in here and I am going right away to look for another place." In a minute, he already would change his mind. He never let me move out. He didn't take a penny rent from me.

I always did try to bring him customers. By then I knew a lot of people working around there. I would see them and ask them, "What are you going to buy?" And I would say, "Come with me, come with me. Frank, I have a new customer for you." I knew their credit was good. "You give him credit," I would tell Frank. "When he will not pay the bill, I will pay the bill." And he did a tremendous business, Frank, like that.

For five years I was in business with Sam Schwartzman. American Byproducts, we called it. We exported second-hand clothing to Europe. Only I couldn't take it. We made a nice living, but it was not for me. A lot of people worked for us; we had machinery, trucks and press machines. I had to be there 8:00 in the morning to open up. And when the people were going home, then I'd have to close the place. This was not for me. I only wanted to work outside, to be outside. I liked to be outside. So, I sold the business and went back to hosiery.

When the hosiery business got more competitive, I heard about something called converters. Some men would buy rejects and sew on the tops and bottoms of the stockings. Converting meant to fix them up.

So I went to Morris and asked if he had rejects. He could give me 10 cartons. I asked Morris the price.

"Forget about it; they are rejects."

"Morris, I don't want just these rejects. I want rejects that you will have tomorrow and next week," I told him.

So he told the girl, "Make him up a bill for just very little money."

Somebody told me if you want rejects you go to the Baird Brothers – Carl and Donald – on Delaware Avenue. I did a lot of business with them, too. Once when I was at their warehouse, Donald called me in. He asked me when I came to this country, and I told him. I didn't want to talk to anybody about anything, because my stories – I'm not a story maker. I found out the best thing is not to talk because my language is no good. People don't understand too much Yiddish. It's better not to talk. And I figured I saw a lot; people cannot understand. So I felt that by talking I'm disturbing myself, and I don't want to be disturbed. I was plenty disturbed; I don't need it anymore.

"I see that you are a man who knows what he is doing," Donald Baird told me one day. "I need the waste from the same rejects." There's always about 40 to 50 percent waste from the rejects. The people who I sell the rejects to, they probably have waste.

I told him to call Joe, his truck driver. I didn't lose any time. A half hour was to me too much. When Joe came back, we loaded up rejects and took them to one of my buyers.

I sold him the rejects and I told him I wanted the waste. He sent a boy and threw bundles of waste on the pavement. We weighed it on the scales, packed up the truck and headed back to Baird's. It was already late; in a minute they would close. When they opened the cartons, they couldn't believe it. I was there three times in that one day – back and forth.

It was summertime, and I was sweating from the heat and from the dust. And I'm dirty like a pig. I came home and took off my clothes, and I jumped in and took a bath to clean myself up. I was so full of dirt; the water was black from the cartons and everything. I didn't realize what sweating was like in the United States. Here is a different climate than in Europe. I cleaned up and I ate supper, and in the morning I was back at the Bairds. They gave me a check and I made a nice profit.

The hell with the hosiery, I decided. I have to go into the waste business.

One day, when I was already in good shape, I got a call from a man named Dave, who was in the waste business. I knew about him. He was a very sharp cookie. And he could take advantage of you. He didn't care about you too much. He asked me to come in. He had something for me, I figured, so I went.

I waited an hour before he saw me. The girl had brought him tea to his table, and he was drinking the tea and eating cookies, and he didn't want to disturb himself by talking to me.

Finally he told me he wanted to sell his 75 gauge hosiery at a very high price. I had a customer in New York who wanted that product, but he wouldn't pay the price. And I wanted to make a nice profit; I didn't want to work for pennies.

I tell him, "Dave, you don't have to sell it through me, you know. There are plenty of customers to sell it. My time is valuable; I cannot lose any time."

When I left, he called another manufacturer and said, "What's the matter with this greenhorn? He tells me that his time is valuable." And he answers him, "Dave, his time is valuable. He is a busy man and he has no time. And he has to make a profit. Without a profit, he is not working."

Dave called me back. He said that I should sell it at the price my customer offered. The New Yorker didn't want to buy from him directly; he insisted I should be in the middle. So I did send him the hosiery, and he did send the money. After that, I didn't want to bother with this.

I did do more business with the Baird Brothers, and I was busy day and night. I had with them a good time. We went to the nightclubs together. I used to come home sometimes drunk. And to get drunk, I had to drink a lot. Sometimes I was drinking too much.

When Du Pont lost its patent for nylon, the waste business became bad. I heard about a new hot item: double-knit stretch. Single knit, if you stretch it, starts to run at the end, but double-knit doesn't run. So I started up with that.

Sophie used to help me. I took her to Allentown. I bought there piece goods, double knit – one yard, two yards. I bought it, sent it to the dyer, the dyer dyed the material. It was delivered and that was it. Sometimes Sophie and I spent the whole day there.

People have a habit, they think, "I don't know something else." But that's not true. Try something else on a small scale and you will learn and you will be in business again.

In the United States, anybody who wants to work can always find it, if he is capable to do it. I used to go away from merchandise not a week but a year before – I saw a year ahead of time that it would be

SIMON AND SOPHIE AT A FAMILY WEDDING, PHILADELPHIA, 1969.

no good. I did that with the hosiery; I did it with the waste. And after half a year, I got out of double-knit stretch. When polyester came out, it completely ruined the double-knit stretch business. So, comes the polyester, and I figure that's enough. And I stopped.

And this is it. Now I'm sitting here thinking, and it doesn't bother me that I'm not in business now. Absolutely not. I'm enjoying my retirement. Should I go back into business now?

No.

SIMON IN ISRAEL, 1967

SIMON'S BROTHER ISAK IN ISRAEL, 1967

LEFT TO RIGHT: SIMON'S SISTER, NECHAMA PEREL, HIS BROTHER ISAK, BROTHER IN-LAW YESHAYAHU PEREL AND SIMON, TOGETHER IN ISRAEL IN 1967. NECHAMA HAD MOVED TO ISRAEL BEFORE THE WAR. ISAK STAYED IN MUNICH, GERMANY AFTER THE WAR.

SIMON AND SOPHIE IN PHILADELPHIA, 1972

SOPHIE STERLING AT HOME IN 1980

17

'Nobody Is Sorry For Me'

There was a man in Poland who I knew very well. His name was Casil Hyman. He had a wife and children. He didn't have much money. I don't know if he was worth all together a couple hundred dollars in American money.

When he made a few pennies, he set out to buy a whole week's supply of eggs from the farmers. He packed the eggs into wooden crates and loaded them on his wagon. He used cut straw to protect them, but the straw was very thin, maybe half an inch thick. He spread it the crates, and then put on the eggs. Again straw, and again some eggs.

He had to drive about 20 miles to the place where he could sell his eggs. Before he got there, he had plenty of broken eggs. He lost more than half the money that the eggs were worth. At this time, they were selling eggs not by the dozen but by the crate, which held about 60 eggs. The prices were changing every moment.

He drove home, broken. He had made a few pennies to buy some eggs, and he lost so much money on them.

As he was driving back to the town, he saw a fire. His family was in that town, so he tried to drive quicker. As he came near the town, he got off his horse and went to look at the fire. The whole town was out looking at the fire.

A little shack that someone used for storing wood was burning. That little shack was worth nothing, maybe 5 dollars. Casil looked and he said to himself, "The whole town is out watching the shack burning. I have troubles. I burned out all my money on the eggs and nobody is near me."

He told me the story a few times. He never could forget. "They are sorry for the little shack. I burned up all my money by the eggs;

nobody is sorry for me."

This story came to my mind when I had a dream last night. I had a dream from the war all the time, and it still didn't stop. I woke up very shaky. I went downstairs and smoked a cigarette. I sat in the chair and I reminded myself about the eggs and the fire, about the whole town coming out to watch the poor little shack.

It reminds me of the survivors' gathering that will be held soon; the people are coming together. It's getting a lot of attention. But Jews were being burned in Europe by the millions and no one looked. Everybody burned up. Nobody was around. Now they're all coming; now the survivors are making a gathering. Will there be entertainment? Will there be speaking? It doesn't appeal to me. But I cannot criticize; I don't know if this is right or wrong.

What percentage from all the people, the survivors, are left? Two percent? Three percent? So the three percent are making a big gathering. In my opinion, they will never be able to explain what was.

I was in a lot of places during the war, and certain places and things I saw people don't even talk about because they were not there. There were no witnesses. For example, near us was a village, Mikolayov; it was far from a railroad. There were a nice few families – Jewish people – living there. The Germans took them out all together to this little mountain. The people dug their own graves. They put the Jews in the hole, except for two people, who they left alive to cover the dead with earth. They shot them. When they finished digging, they shot those two people also. Nobody knows about this. Nothing. And this was happening in thousands of villages.

Nobody talks about this. They only talk about the ghetto from Warsaw, and about Treblinka or Auschwitz or Majdanek, where the majority who lived were. Hundreds of thousands of people were shot down like this.

I do remember this. When I was in a camp in Zloczow, the Germans took out the people from the Brody ghetto. But they didn't take them to Treblinka or Auschwitz. They took them out in the woods. Four or five weeks before, they had prepared big holes, but nobody knew it. They took them from the ghetto out there by truck and they shot them in the holes. Sophie told me about it, and I heard the same story from a few other survivors who were in the Brody ghetto. At that time, there were maybe about 12,000 Jewish people living there. When they finished, when they killed all the Jews around there, they liquidated. They cleaned up the place; everything, and the farmers had to go work on this ground – like nothing.

Near us, there was a town, Beresteczko. There were a nice few thousand Jewish people. People don't even know that this town once existed with Jewish people. Beresteczko, and a Lopatin and a Radziechov. In Radziechov, there was already a railroad station, so they loaded them up and took them to Belzec.

Nobody even talked about Belzec. Hundreds of thousands of Polish Jews from my village and nearby towns were taken to Belzec. My father was there, and my two sisters were there with their children. The Germans exterminated them there, and they burned up their bodies. In Auschwitz, the people were working. In Belzec, they weren't working. The Germans took them there by train. They got off the train and the same day they were liquidated.

At Belzec, after they killed all the Jews, they took all the buildings down and destroyed the camp. They planted pine trees to hide it. No sign. No sign. As if nothing had existed there.

I was a year in the woods. I had no information about what was going on, but I knew that around me, there were no Jewish people, except the few who were in the woods. I never did believe that I would be alive and I would see with my eyes another Jewish person. When the Russians freed me, I went to these old towns: Radzivillov, Dubno, Lutsk, Minsk. I didn't see anybody there – no Jewish people, no Jewish people. And there had been hundreds of thousands of Jews.

From this they don't talk, you know. And this bothers me. They should ask, "Where are the people?"

Later, when I came back to Cracow after the war, I saw some of the people from Auschwitz and from the other camps. I couldn't believe it, that I would see any survivors from there. You should have seen them, how they all looked. I saw some girls who looked liked old women. Their faces. . . their hair was cut or they had no hair. And they were still wearing the uniform with the stripe.

At any gathering, some people will be talking. But where are the people from Lemberg? Where are the Jews from Dubno? From Lutsk? It's unbelievable.

Anton Lukasiewicz died a number of years ago. From the first month that I came to the United States, I had been sending the family money, and I never stopped. When Lukasiewicz was living, I sent the money to him, and when he died, I sent it to his wife. When she moved to Canada – she had a sister there – I sent it to his son, who was maybe 17 or 18 when I was in Poland. I never stopped it. When I first came here, I started sending 5 dollars every two months. Then I increased it, and just a couple of weeks ago, I sent him some money.

He doesn't actually get the money. I send the dollars to a Polish organization, and they give him a slip. There is a store in Poland, where they sell American merchandise, and he can use the slip to buy things in the store.

Some years ago, I wrote to Lukasiewicz. I asked him to ask if Stanislaw Mazak, the Polish priest who had been so kind to me, if he needed something. I also sent him a gold cross. Lukasiewicz wrote back that the priest wanted a reed for his nephew's clarinet. He couldn't get it in Poland, so I sent him some reeds. That's all he wanted.

Recently, I got a letter from Anton's son. He wrote that somebody had informed the Polish government that Mazak, the priest, had helped some Jewish people in the wartime. So the government gave him a medal and a gold cross. When he retires, they will increase his pension on account of this. Mazak was a fine gentleman, a fine man.

If at least 20 percent of the people in Poland had been like Mazak, there would be a lot of Jewish survivors. But it was a very small percentage. A very, very small percentage.

SIMON'S DAUGHTER PHYLLIS, WITH FRANKA LUKASIEWICZ
AT THE CEREMONY HONORING HER AND HER LATE HUSBAND,
ANTON, AS "RIGHTEOUS AMONG THE NATIONS" BY YAD VASHEM,
SASKATOON, CANADA, 1990.

EPILOGUE

Here in the United States, I was in business. I was connected with a lot of people. I never had trouble with anybody. And I always tried my best. I tried to act like everybody here because you cannot act . . .

Only when I came home, and I was by myself, I was an altogether different person. I never was a good sleeper. My mind right away came to pictures of the war. Day and night, and day and night, and day and night.

In a dream a couple of nights ago, the Germans were running after me with their guns open. They caught a lot of Jewish people. The Jews were running and running, and the Germans were beating them. I, because I always was an escaper, was escaping again. They were after me, and I was so strong and young and I was jumping on different kinds of dangerous places. It took a long time. And the last second when they were close to me, I woke up.

I looked at the clock. It was 2:00 in the morning, 10 after 2. I was breathing so hard. I went down and I smoked three cigarettes in the night, and I couldn't go back to bed.

I did get back in bed at 4:30. I lay down for a minute – and I got up again. I walked around, I looked at the paper, and I got back in bed. I got up. I read the paper. I looked out the window; it didn't help. I looked out the window, waiting for the day to come. Close to 5:00 I lay down and I fell asleep for an hour.

This goes on very often. It never stops. Never stops. When I talk to people like me, they have the same things, the same bad dreams.

Then comes the morning. You go out to see the people. It's not that I don't want to tell them. They cannot understand. They will look at me like I am narrow-minded or something. So I don't tell anybody. Because what they will know? Because they don't know anything.

Actually, they know a lot about other things. Only they don't know what went on. I belong here in my building to a men's club. Very nice people, everybody. We talk about a lot of things. But I don't talk to them about this, because they are not interested to know. And if I would tell them, they will not understand what I am talking about. Do you understand?

So, I am better off not to talk.

Letters From Föhrenwald Displaced Persons' Camp

January 5, 1945

Dear Nechama,

I, my wife Sophie and our brother, Isak, remained alive by some miracle that we don't understand. The cursed Hitler – it is impossible to send you any details. Our happiness will be great if we receive a letter from you and your husband. Sister, when you get this letter, please send us a telegram immediately. I want to know whether you are alive. We are in Lemberg. Write to us at the address I am giving you. As soon as I get a letter from you, I'll write you more details. Fourteen of us from our town remain alive with broken hearts. Sister, please do whatever possible so that we get a letter from you soon.

I send kisses to you, my dear ones.

Your brother, Simon

December 6, 1946

Dear Sister,

On the first of November, we received your letter that you are well. But, dear sister, our date of leaving here is still not known. It looks like we will still have to wait. We have cousins who want to bring us to America. They are the Bodek family from our dear mother's side and also our cousin, Sam Gross. He is our dear father's sister's son. We are doing everything we can that is possible to go to America. We received letters from our cousins, and because of those letters, dear sister, we have not lost hope.

I gather from your letter that you did not get the letter in which I wrote who remained alive, who survived from our town of Szczurowice. Surviving is Mendel Friedman and his son, Isak; Pina Potash and her two children, Mendle and Motle; Jacob Potash; Fishel Fisch; Mani Fisch; Yossel Parnas; Besse Gold; Shmuel Felder; Michael Reiss and Layke Reiss. We were told that Sherman Moses is alive and waiting with the Russian military. That we remained alive, we don't understand. Can you imagine that only around 50 Jewish people remained alive from Radziechov? Even fewer. Maybe five or six remained alive from Beresteczko.

Dear sister, we beg you write at least one letter every week. Perhaps you are angry because I have not written recently. Right after our daughter Faigela was born, she became quite sick and I had to take her to the hospital. The hospital is 30 kilometers away, and every day I had to travel that distance. It lasted for four months, and now, this week, I have taken her home. Thank God, she is well.

Now, just imagine my pain. I would by now also have had a son, 10 years old. But it is awful; they tore him from out of my hands. There is a great deal to tell about this, but I simply can't. My mind will not accept this most valuable thing that we lost.

Michael, Sophie's brother, also has a daughter. Her name is Baille Charna, named after their mother and Charna Singer.

Heartfelt regards to your husband and children. My best greetings and kisses.

Simon

September 22, 1947

Dear Nechama,

We have received your letter, and just as you would like to see us, we also want to see you. You are now our only sister. You ask whether it will take much more time before we will be able to leave here. Unfortunately, we don't know that exactly, but we feel confident that it won't take much longer. Everything has its own end, and this also must come to an end.

We are very worried about the unrest that takes place in our country, Israel. From the latest news it seems that things will quiet down and you will be able to live in peace in the Jewish homeland. In any case, we want you to be cautious and not to go out into the streets unless absolutely necessary. We are, thank God, all well. Simon and Sophie's daughter is fine and wonderful.

Dear sister, we ask you one more time, please be careful. It's better to suffer a little and wait for the bad times to pass, instead of endangering oneself. Don't worry about us. We manage to get by somehow.

We send regards and kiss you all.

Isak

January 17, 1948

Dear Nechama,

Finally, we are able to correspond with you. We don't have to tell you that we follow the news three times every day to find out what is happening in the land of Israel. Unfortunately, lately there has been much bad news. We are concerned and very much worried about everybody, but especially you in your circumstances. We feel badly that we wrote so little to warn you about how you should behave in such a serious and dangerous time. Unfortunately, we had much experience of this during the time of great upheaval and again, unfortunately, we learned a lot from it. We realize that there is no comparison as to what we went through to what is happening now in Israel, but we know that one has to protect oneself wherever one can. Be prepared with lots of stored food, and don't go into the street unnecessarily. We hope that it will all end soon with a satisfactory ending.

Please write to us frequently so that we will know what is happening to you. We are well, send kisses to all of you, and wish to hear good news from you.

Isak and Simon

August 20, 1948

My Dear Ones,

You can't imagine the pleasure your letter gave us. We worry about you and the situation in Israel. But thank God, as long as one is alive, one is fine. We are very frightened because we are people who have had great pain. It is so very wonderful to hear from you.

We have a very sweet daughter, Faigela. She takes after your mother. She got a present today from Isak, so now she says she loves only Isak. She says everything. She is our only comfort.

Please excuse me that I write so little to you. I am very much alone. The others go away Sunday and don't get back until Friday for the Shabbat weekend. They try to make a living because the amount of money that we get for one week lasts us only for one day. It is boring to have to struggle for such a long time. But God willing, we have come through so much already; we will also survive this dull camp and get out of Germany.

I write with one hand while I hold my child with my other arm. She is a good child, and our only consolation.

We send kisses to you and your children.

Sophie

December 1, 1948

My Dear Ones,

I cannot possibly write to you about what excitement your last letter brought to us. It is now three months since we heard a word from you, and with all the trouble that you are having in Israel, we were worried.

We have high hopes that our leaving here for America will take place quite soon. It is now very boring living in this camp, and we are anxious to leave. I hope you understand why we want to go to America where we found family. They have intervened in several ways on our behalf and have prepared a place for us to live. In spite of the fact that we want very much to go, we are in doubt and feel demoralized. We have hope that you will come to see us in America, or we will be able to come from America to see you in Israel. Isak is writing you a separate letter.

We send you best wishes and kisses.

Your brother, Simon

February 16, 1949

Dear Nechama,

I got a letter from Simon the very first day of his arrival to our cousin's home in Philadelphia. He didn't write much except to say that the family are very good people. I'm sure you will be getting a letter from him. It gives me great pleasure to hear that you are well and that your children are playing with the newborn.

Since it happened that Simon and his family already left, it doesn't matter to me any more when I leave. I am living in Munich, have a nice apartment and also am earning money. With Simon, it was different. He lived in the displaced persons' camp, and you can imagine what the circumstances were.

I am very disturbed that I didn't have the opportunity to come and see you in Israel. Unfortunately, I didn't have the money. It costs $300 and that is difficult for me right now. I hope that the first opportunity I have, I'll visit you from America, and see the land of Israel. That is a hope I have not given up.

Let us all live and be well.

Isak

Isak lived in Munich until 1972. In his final days he went to Tel Aviv to be cared for by his sister, Nechama. His is buried in Israel.

A Daughter's Epilogue

It was only in the mid eighties that Holocaust survivors were beginning to be widely encouraged to tell and record their stories. Since then many survivors have found comfort in knowing that others are willing to struggle to understand what they experienced, and they are anxious to leave testimony which holds enduring lessons for this and future generations. I hope that as my father shared his story with me, he felt a piece of the heaviness lifted. Certainly, publishing this book has done that for me. My parents would be very gratified knowing, as I am, that this book serves as a memorial to those lost. We remember them.

I am grateful that my parents had a network of survivor friends who exchanged stories over endless card games, and never had to explain how they felt. They became extended family. Through my close connections with other children of survivors I am forunate to have a community where we share a language requiring few words.

As the bearer of my family's legacy, I carry heartache, pride and responsibility. In my journey to find peace with my family's history, an important first step was to acknowledge my own personal losses. As a child I always felt that my issues were trivial in light of my parents' experiences. I needed to acknowledge that although I never knew the family I lost, my losses are real. I needed to begin to mourn the brother, grandparents, aunts, uncles and cousins with whom I would have shared my life.

Another important step in my search for peace with my family's history was to meet and honor members of the Lukasiewicz family, who at enormous risk, extended a lifeline to my parents. While growing up, I had heard their names spoken so often and noticed

My father and I in Philadelphia in 1950, a year after my family immigrated to the United States, Philadelphia, 1950.

My father, Simon Sterling at my wedding,   February 1986.

the special attention my parents gave their letters. After Anton Lukasiewicz passed away, Franka, his wife, moved to Saskatoon, Canada to live near her granddaughter. In July of 1990, I flew to Canada, where I met Franka and her family. I had previously sent documents recommending that Anton and Franka be honored by Yad Vashem, an organization in Israel that recognizes rescuers during the Holocaust.

During my visit, Toronto's Consul General of Israel awarded Franka and her late husband, Anton, the "Righteous Among the Nations" award in a ceremony attended by her family, friends and members of her community. Participating in this ceremony was a magical event.

Perhaps the most difficult step in my journey was to bring my parents' story to light through this book. Some stories take a long time. With this sacred mission accomplished, I hope to honor my parents and all those whose stories will never be told. May their memory be a blessing.

PHYLLIS STERLING JACOBS
FEBRUARY, 2005

MY COUSIN BETTY RICE (MICHAEL'S DAUGHTER) AND I, MAY 2004.

MY FAMILY-MY HUSBAND MARC AND DAUGHTERS SARA AND SIMONE (LEFT) CELEBRATING SIMONE'S BAT MITZVAH, MAY 2002.